ST HELENS
Knowsley
Knowsley Park
Knowsley Hall
Croxteth Hall
Norris Green
West Derby
LIVERPOOL
Woolfall Heath
PRESCOT
HUYTON
ROBY
Page Moss
Dovecot
Knotty Ash
Broad Green
Wavertree Nook
Olive Mount
Childwall
Gateacre
Calderstones
Woolton
Allerton
Aigburth
Garston
Hunt's Cross
Halewood
Halewood Green
Tarbock
Tarbock Green
Tarbock Hall
Whiston
Whiston Lane Ends
Rainhill
Rainhill Stoops
Cronton
Farnworth
WIDNES
Ditton
Hough Green
Hale Bank
Ditton Junc Sta
Eccleston
Eccleston Park
Thatto Heath
Peasley Cross
Sutton
Sutton Leach
Sutton Manor
Clock Face
Bold
Bold Heath
Cuerdley Cross
Appleton
Simm's Cross
West Bank
Runcorn Gap
Blackbrook
Gerard's Bridge
Denton's Green
St Helens Junc Sta
Huyton Park
Golf Course
Pex Hill
Town End
Upton
Barrow's Green
Whitfield's Cross
Shell Green
Lugsdale
Moss Bank
The Hempstones
Marshgate
Sewage Works
St Helens Canal
Ditton Brook
Halsnead Park
Windy Arbor
Prince's Ho
Blundell's Hill
Tower College
Mill Green
South Lane
Doe Green
Power Station
CUERDLEY
Works

MSC 571056

LIVERPOOL and Merseyside

THIS IS YOUR REGION

LIVERPOOL AND MER

Other titles in the
THIS IS YOUR CITY
AND THIS IS YOUR REGION SE

- GLASGOW AND THE CLYDE
- LONDON
- MANCHESTER
- CARDIFF

In preparation:

- BIRMINGHAM
- NEWCASTLE-UPON-TYNE

HOLMES McDOUGALL, EDINBURGH EH7 5AL

Contents

ISBN 7157 1042-7

Gerard Bailey
Bob Jones (Editor)
George Lucy
Jim Lyon
designed and illustrated by
Anthony Lee Ross MSIA

This is your region LIVERPOOL AND MERSEYSIDE

First Glimpse

Every day passengers fly into **Speke Airport.** As the airliners coast over the River Mersey with their landing lights flashing, the passengers see Merseyside spread out below them. The River snakes its way inland, and on its banks the cranes of the ship-building yards in Birkenhead reach out into the sky. On both sides of the Mersey the shapes of the docks can be seen with hundreds of ships from all over the world lying at their berths.

Each airliner swings in a circle over the City of Liverpool, past the Pier Head and the bold Liver Birds perched on The Royal Liver Building. Below the rows of houses, the city streets, the parks and schools form a patchwork of a living city. Soon the wheels touch down and the passengers climb down the steps, walk across to the Airport Buildings and clear customs. They are soon on their way by road through the suburbs on the eight mile journey to Liverpool.

A mixture of old and new flashes past. Rows of old terraced houses stand side by side with the new gleaming high rise flats. The first impression is one of a changing world.

Eventually the city buildings tower high above the busy streets. The journey is over. The visitors have arrived in Liverpool, the centre of Merseyside. This is a large, exciting city.

Aerial view of Liverpool.

Theme A Merseyside now and then

A1. Growing all the time

Two million people live on Merseyside. Not all live in Liverpool although it is the most important centre in the area.

It has taken a long time for Merseyside's population to grow to two million. In the year 1272 there were only 840 people living in Liverpool. As the port grew in importance so the population has increased. It was only in 1699 that Liverpool was considered important enough to be separated from the nearby parish of **Walton,** which is now part of Liverpool. In 1699 the population was only 2000, but by 1801 a hundred and two years later, it had increased to 79 777.

Every ten years the Government carries out a census to find out how many people live in Britain. A census was held in 1971. The following graph gives the population growth of Liverpool since 1801.

You will notice that between 1831 and 1861 the population rose quickly. This was because thousands of Irish people fled from Ireland because the potato crop failed.

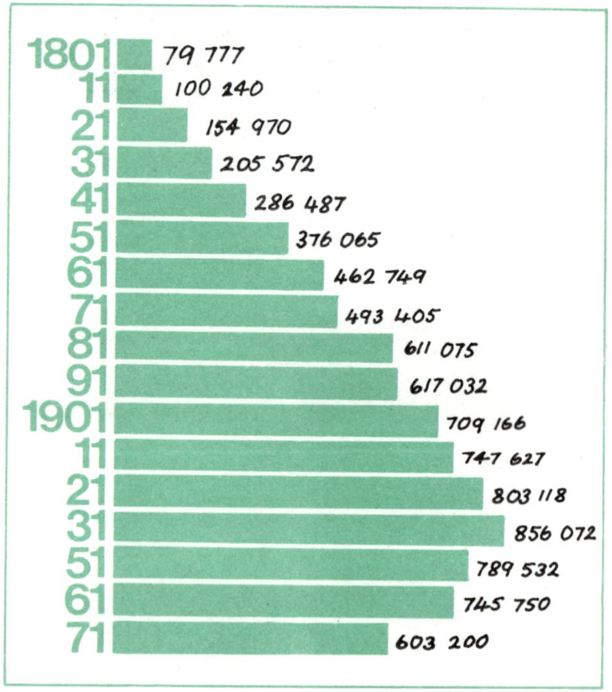

Houses

They settled in Liverpool because it was the major port to which Irish people could travel. Most were too poor to be able to travel further in Britain. They settled on the spot. To accommodate such vast numbers houses had to be built quickly. This table shows how many houses there were in Liverpool and suburbs in the census years 1831–1861.

No. of houses

1831–40	1841–50	1851-60	1861–70
34 378	45 385	59 556	75 189

In Liverpool within the city itself today there are 61 120 Corporation houses, 81 170 rented houses other than the Corporation houses and 62 210 owner occupied houses. This makes a total of 205 500 dwellings.

As more houses have been built, living conditions have become less crowded over the last hundred years. In 1861 there were an average of 6·1 persons in every house. In 1961 there were an average of 3·6 for every house.

Find out when your house was built. Look out for man-hole covers which may have the date they were made on them. Some houses also display the date they were built over the door or on some part of the walls. Look at other buildings in your neighbourhood. You will find clues to tell you how old the property is.

Shipping

More people came to Liverpool because it was a port. As shipping grew so did the trade. With the growth of trade more people came in search of a steady job and homes for their families.

In 1565 there were only fifteen ships belonging to Liverpool shipowners and their tonnage was 259 tonnes. The numbers grew steadily as this → chart shows.

By the year 1752, ships from Liverpool were sailing and trading all over the Western Hemisphere. In 1752, the following numbers of ships sailed from Liverpool:—

Growth of shipping 1565-1701

	Ships	Tonnes
1565	15	259
1648	24	462
1709	84	5 187

Ships sailing from Liverpool 1752

Here you can see by how much sea trade has increased in the past 120 or so years. These figures show the increase of shipping.

1855	4 096 160 tonnes
1905	15 996 387 tonnes
1955	26 158 954 tonnes

As steam took the place of sail and motor vessels replaced steam, goods could travel at greater speeds and in larger quantities.

Roads

Another increase on Merseyside which can be measured is in the increase of motor cars on the roads. The motor car has affected the world we live in. The number of cars in Britain over the past years has grown rapidly as this shows:—

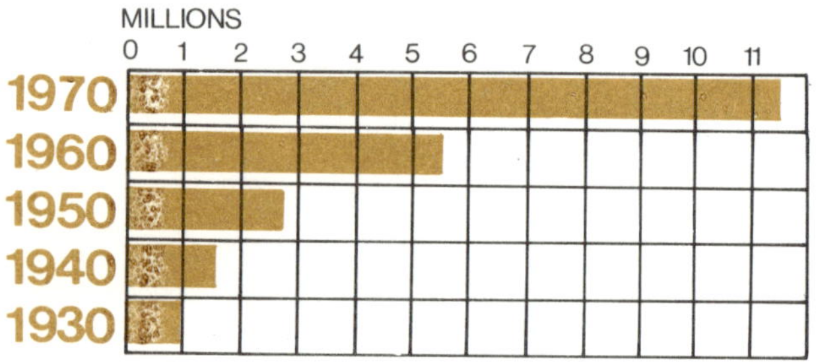

By the year 1980 17 million cars are expected to be on the roads of this country. This is why you are seeing so many roads being altered on Merseyside and the appearance of flyovers in Liverpool and Birkenhead. New tunnels under the Mersey have become a necessity. The number of cars using the **Queensway Tunnel** which was opened in 1934 shows how the roads have become more and more congested.
It is not surprising that the shape of the centres of Merseyside towns is being changed to accommodate so many extra cars.

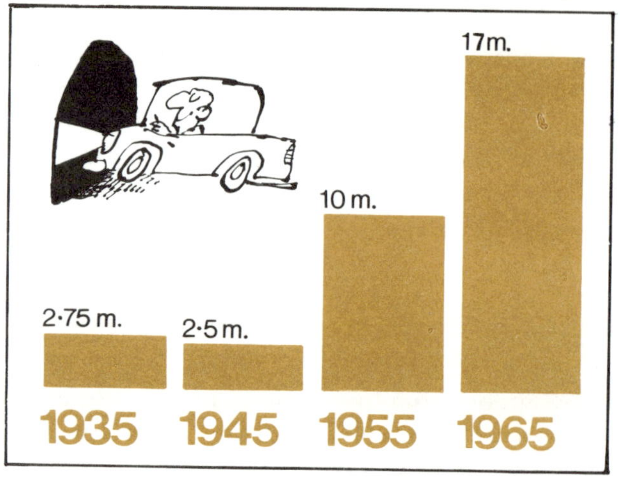

The Queensway Tunnel.

A2. The beginnings of Merseyside

If you see any roadworks on Merseyside, you will see the red sandstone rock which is just below the surface. Most of the local churches and the **Anglican Cathedral** have been built in this stone.

Sandstone has been made from sand. Millions of years ago it was at the bottom of the sea. The weight of the water and the silt compressed the sand and set it solid. As the earth grew older the surface was twisted and compressed. These giant forces bent, cracked and finally pushed the newly formed sandstone rocks right out of the sea. Some were pushed so high that they formed hills.

These red sandstone hills of Merseyside are found at Thurstaston, Wallasey, Bidston and Bebington in the Wirral, and Mossley Hill, Woolton, Everton and Breeze Hill on the Lancashire side. The layer of rock is quite thick as you can see if you travel by train through the deep railway cuttings between Edge Hill and Lime Street Station.

Edge Hill cutting.

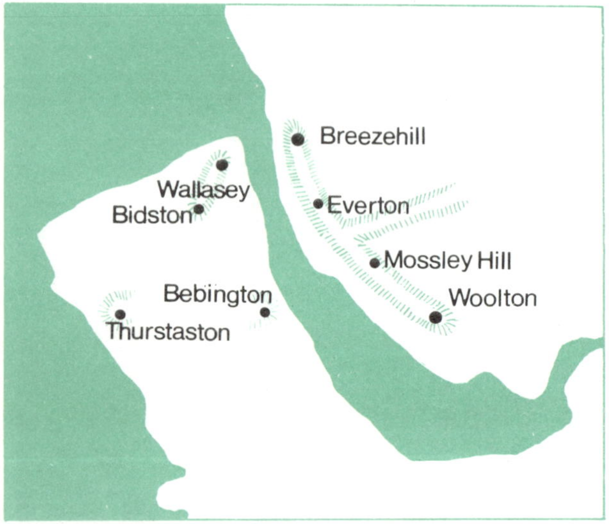

Fossils of footprints left by prehistoric animals have been found in the sandstone of Storeton Quarry in the Wirral. These footprints, made when the rock was still sand, are 200 million years old.

The hills of Merseyside, newly emerged from the sea by some vast earthquake, began to get their coating of soil. There was some silt from the bottom of the sea which dried out but there was also the effect of hot days and cold nights which broke up rocks into fine grains of soil.

Then the weather got colder. The whole of the Northern British Isles became one enormous ice cap. The ice pushed further south in great glaciers. Down the Irish Sea came a mighty river of ice carrying with it boulders, sand and mud.

At times the ice was 2000 feet thick and as it moved forward it scratched and scoured the rocks over which it travelled.

Eventually the weather became warmer and the glaciers stopped advancing. When the ice began to melt in the Merseyside area, its load of boulders, pebbles and mud settled. One such boulder can still be seen in Coronation Park, Crosby. It weighs over eighteen tonnes. It was carried by the ice from Scotland.

Take a walk around your area and collect as many different kinds of stones as you can. Your geography teacher will be able to identify them for you. Keep a good look out especially for the red sandstone rocks which are typical of Merseyside.

Above: The hills of Merseyside.
Right: Fossilised footprint of Chinotnerium at Storeton Quarry.

First Inhabitants

After all these recent upheavals, and they are recent when we think of 200 million years, Merseyside settled down to the familiar shape we know today. The first inhabitants have left few traces but we find out something from the names they gave places. The Ancient Britons or the Welsh have left their mark in such names as Liscard (Welsh, llys—hall giving the full meaning 'Hall on the cliff') and Ince (Welsh, ynys—an island).
The Romans have given us Dee which comes from **Deva,** the Roman name for Chester. (Deva, the river, was considered to be the waters of a goddess.)
When the first Anglo-Saxons came they found the Ancient Britons or the Welsh occupying certain sites. Their word for the Welsh was Walla and from this came Walton (the place of the Welsh) and Wallasey (the island of the Welsh).
"Ham" (village) and "burn" (stream) have generally come down from Anglo-Saxon. These Anglo-Saxon invaders came from across the North Sea. They landed on the East coast and slowly spread across to Merseyside.
Another group of invaders who came later were the Norsemen from Scandinavia. They sailed into the Irish Sea having gone round Northern Scotland and spread inland from the coast. In these Norse place names we find:
"by"—a place or village;
"kirk"—a church;
"beck"—a stream;
"breck"—an edge;
"meols"—a sandhill
and "dale"—a valley.
Look at a map of Merseyside and pick out all the places that include any of these names. You may like to set them out under different columns, e.g. Welsh, Anglo-Saxon, etc.
Most of these villages were on the high ground around Merseyside. They relied on farming for a living. Liverpool itself was merely a collection of huts. The Roman port of Chester was used for all traffic in the Irish Sea.

Liverpool's Beginnings

Many ships sailed from Chester but the River Dee was silting up so **King John,** who wanted a port for Ireland, turned to Liverpool. On the 28th August 1207 he granted a charter to the town, giving the people great privileges. They could buy and sell what they wanted without paying tolls. They could elect their own sheriffs and govern themselves, and they could also have their own local courts of justice.
Why did the River Dee silt up and not the River Mersey? Find out what has happened to once flourishing ports on the Dee like Parkgate.
About an acre of land was given to the villeins who were once considered unfree men, and they were given their freedom by King John. By Tudor times, when **Henry VIII** was King, Liverpool had grown. The population was about 3000 at that time. Leland (1506–1552), a librarian to the King, was sent on a tour of England in 1536. He wrote of the town:
"Lyrpul, alias Lyverpoole, a paved town hath but a chapel, Walton four miles off.
The King hath a castle there, and the Earl of Derby hath a stone house there.
Irish merchants come much hither as to a good haven. At Lyrpul is small custom paid that causeth merchants to resort thither".
It was this 'good haven' and the 'small custom' that was to lead to the great growth of trade.

A roundship c. 1470.

A3. The growth of trade

The first country to have a trading link with Liverpool was Ireland. Small ships carried salt, alum, coal, barley, malt and hops to Dublin and brought back tallow, hides and linen from Ireland. By 1586 a historian of the time called Camden wrote:

"The Mersey . . . falls into the ocean with a wide channel . . . from a water extending like a pool—very convenient to trade where opens to view Litherpole, commonly called Lirpoole . . . where is the most convenient and most frequented passage to Ireland".

The name Liverpool was spelled in many different ways as you can see from Leland and Camden. Some people think it came from the name of a man, Leofhere, who lived by the pool. Others think it came from an old English word Lifrig, which means muddy or foul. Yet others suggest it comes from old Norse Lither; a slope. Nobody now knows. A similar mystery surrounds the Liver bird. When Liverpool was granted a charter the burgesses decided it was important enough to have a seal for their documents. It is possible that the Eagle of St. John was chosen as a compliment to King John. The eagle held in its beak a sprig of *planta genista*—the plantagenet emblem. Later in 1668 the bird was thought to be a sea cormorant or lever holding a branch of sea weed or laver in its beak. This bird is still in the arms of the city and a pair bestride the Liver Buildings. The Eagle of St. John is found in the arms of the bishopric of the city.

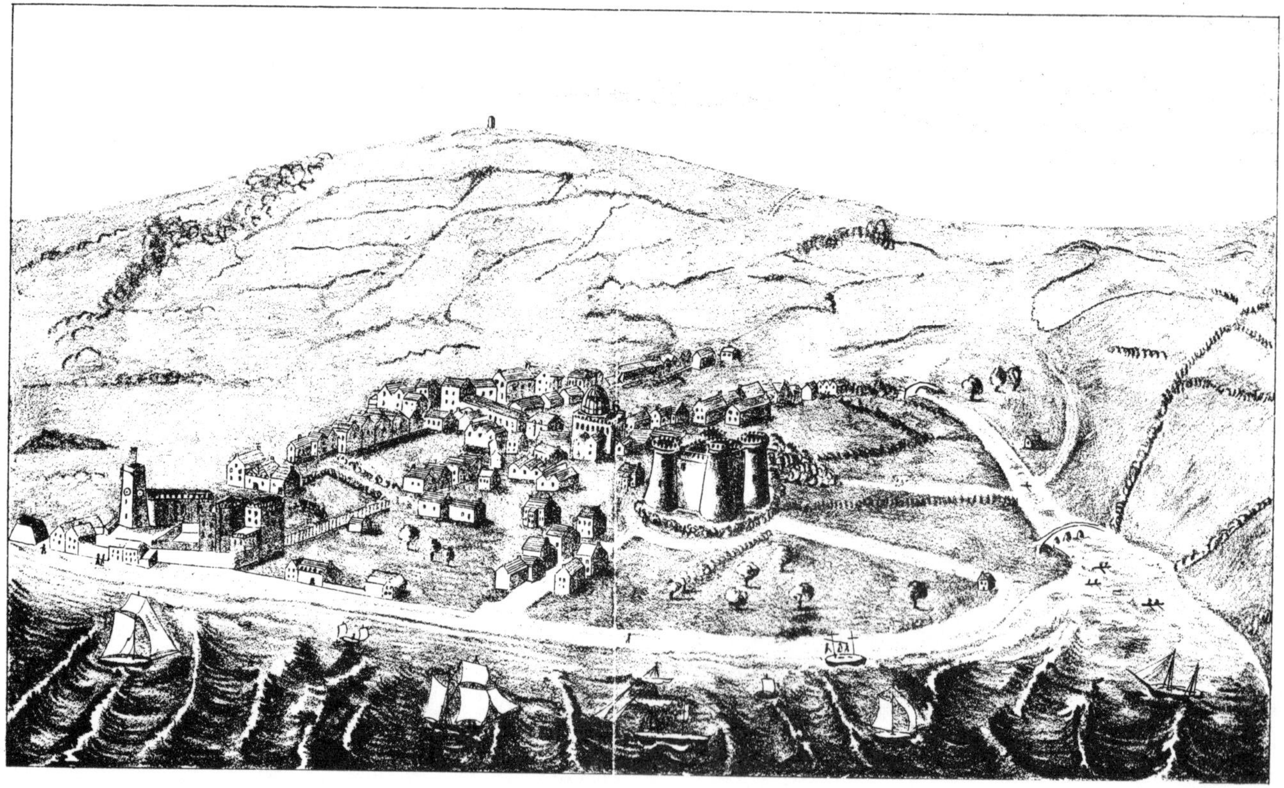

An early view of Liverpool.

The pool is no longer to be seen today. It has been filled in. Its passage is marked today from the Mersey Tunnel entrance (Queensway) along Whitechapel and Paradise Street to join the River where Canning Place now is. The print above shows what early Liverpool looked like. This pool made a safe harbour for ships and the river itself was deep allowing large ships to pass easily. These ships started venturing further from Liverpool. In a document of 1592 there is a note which limits the price of oranges arriving on French ships to 12 pence per 120. This shows that ships as early as this were trading with places further afield than Ireland.

"America, America!—The New World"

But it is not to the continent that Liverpool owes its growth. The opening up of the New World to trade meant that ports on the west coast of Britain became important.
About the middle of the 17th century salt deposits in Cheshire were discovered and began to be mined. The salt was carried to Dungeon Point to be refined. Coal used in the heating part of this process was brought from the nearby coalfield. There was a plentiful supply of clean salt water from the river which was used to refine the salt.
The sea water dissolved the rock salt which came from Cheshire. The liquid was then filtered and the impurities which did not dissolve were left behind. The sea water containing the dissolved salt was heated over coal fires. This drove off the water and left the salt.
Salt was needed to preserve meat: so it was therefore much in demand and became a very valuable export. It was exported as far afield as the New World especially the West Indies.
The ships which sailed from Liverpool at this time carried cargoes of salt and woollen goods. They brought back sugar, rum, and molasses from the West Indies. Sugar was very valuable and was sold for high prices. The first sugar refinery was set up in 1668.
Trade with the colonies in North America continued to expand. Tobacco and turpentine were brought over in large quantities from Virginia. This importing and exporting brought wealth to the town. Merchants became rich.

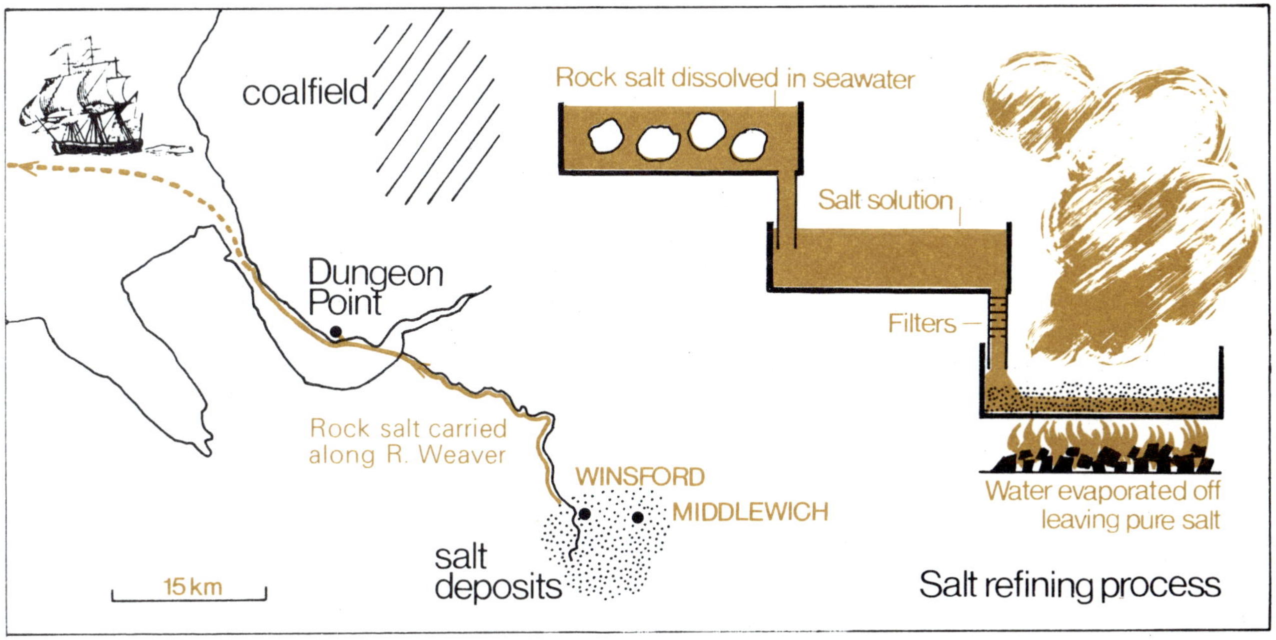

Some of the profits were used to improve the port. In 1693 the first charts of the River Mersey were made to help ships find a safe channel into port and out again. Then in the early years of the eighteenth century the marshy upper reaches of the pool were filled in and the River end of 'Sea Lake' was made into a wet dock. The sailing ships found that strong tides in the river were too high for the anchors to reach the bottom. The pool itself was becoming silted up. Thomas Steers, the engineer who constructed the first dock, had no easy task. The pool had to be dammed and the stream from inland, diverted. The dock was about as big as two football pitches. It was very successful and soon other docks were constructed.
The Mersey Docks and Harbour Company's Education Officer will be able to give you a plan of all the docks on the Liverpool water front.
Construct a model of the port of Liverpool, showing all the docks and indicating when they were built.

Trade With Africa

In 1700 the first ship sailed from Liverpool to Africa. Then more and more ships made their way to the West Coast of Africa. By 1737, 30 ships were sailing to the same destination and by 1752 the number had grown to 83. And what did all these ships carry?—Human beings, slaves from Africa. This was the start of the Slave Trade. Liverpool competed with Bristol and then outrivalled that city which hitherto had been Britain's No. 1 port.
Between 1783 and 1793 Liverpool ships carried 303 737 slaves valued at £13 186 850! Liverpool was now the largest slave trading port in Britain. Cargoes of cheap goods were shipped to West Africa and bartered for slaves. The slaves were then taken in the emptied ships to the West Indies and sold. With the money made at this venture, sugar, rum and spices were bought and brought back to Liverpool. Here are some of the instructions given to the Captain of a slave ship by the owner:

To Captain Hayston. "Liverpool 8th June 1757

You are to proceed (to) the coast of Africa where you must barter your cargo for young slaves or negroes, none under four feet. When you have finished your trade on the coast of Africa endeavour to make the island of Tobago and Jamaica. There apply to Messrs. Hibbert and Millan for disposal of your negroes. Load your vessels in the hold with sugar and between decks with cotton. Your business being done there make the best of your way home".

An End to Slavery

At the end of the eighteenth century, consciences were stirring: this inhuman traffic was under attack. The Quakers were first to campaign against it and other people joined with them until in 1807 slavery was abolished by Act of Parliament. **William Wilberforce** sponsored the Act of Parliament but a local M.P. **William Roscoe** did much to help. Of course it made him very unpopular with the wealthy and powerful slave traders of Liverpool.
With the slave trade abolished, these traders thought the end had come. They expected grass to grow in the streets, the docks to become fish ponds and their fine houses to decay. This did not happen. Four years after the Act, in 1811, the tonnage entering the port had doubled to 611 190 tonnes.

Above: Many slaves died on the voyage in cramped conditions like these.
Right: Areas of Africa from where slaves were taken.

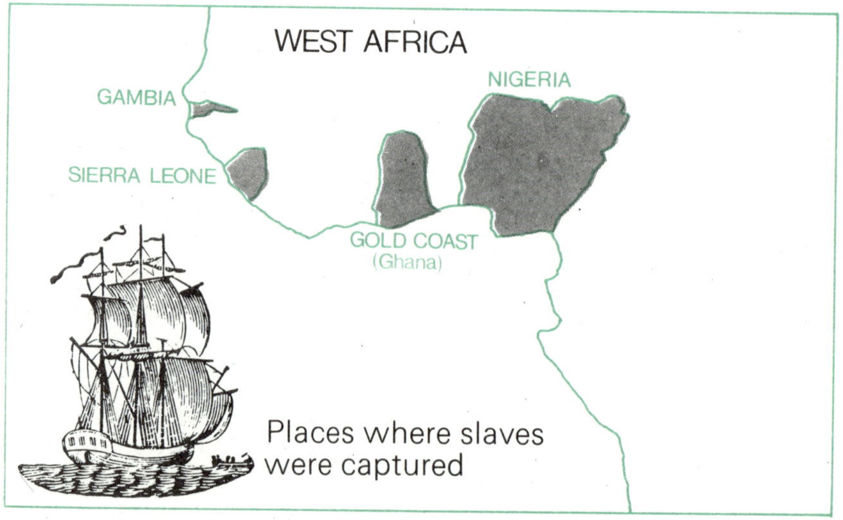

Cotton

This miracle, for so it seemed, was due to the rise of the cotton industry. As it expanded it made Lancashire famous throughout the world. It gave to Liverpool a monopoly of cotton imports and exports which filled the trade gap left by slavery. By 1850 Liverpool's imports amounted to £38 000 000. Of this amount, £16 000 000 were for cotton. (The total value of imports into Britain in the same year was £100 000 000.)

In 1844, 223 318 bales of cotton were imported in ONE WEEK, and one export cargo of 3 000 000 metres of cloth for Hong Kong was worth £45 025. To move this quantity of material, a good transport system was needed.

Towards the end of the 18th century canals had been constructed all over the area.

The LEEDS–LIVERPOOL CANAL joined the port with the woollen towns of Yorkshire. The **Bridgewater,** the **Sankey,** the **Trent** and **Mersey,** the **Shropshire Union** and the **Weaver Navigation** all linked Liverpool with the industries that were growing up in their areas.

But travel by land was still slow because the roads were poor. It still took four days to reach London by stagecoach. The countryside between Liverpool and Manchester, the headquarters of the cotton industry, was very difficult. In 1830 a railway was completed between the two towns. The engineers had had to overcome many difficulties like crossing marshy land. The railway carried 480 000 passengers during its first year. One engine, 'The Planet', did the journey in an hour.

Goods could now travel quickly and smoothly between the cities, increasing in quantity all the time.

Left: The Leeds–Liverpool canal.
Below: The Planet.

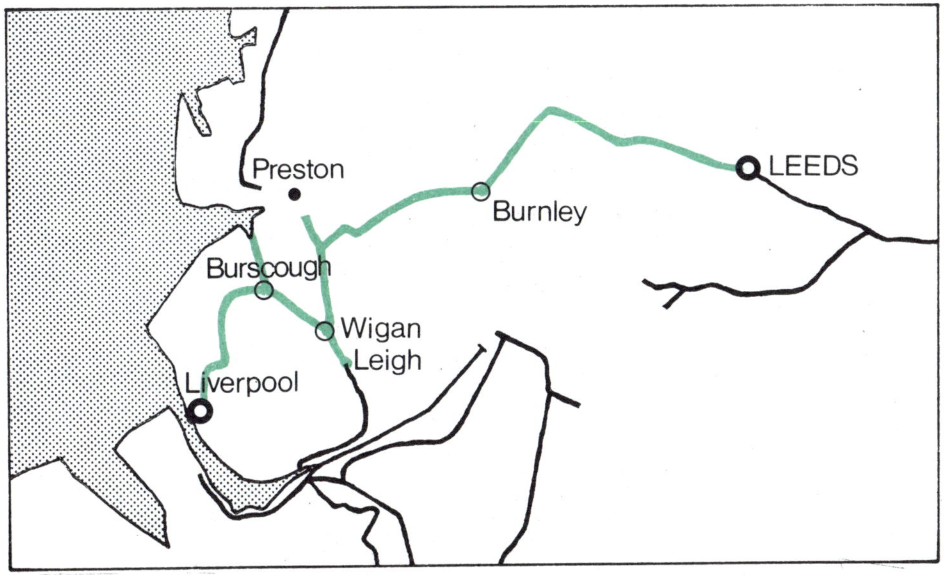

Rubber

The growth of the rubber trade with South America also makes interesting reading. Try reading all about the links set up by the **Booth Line** between Liverpool and Manaos in Brazil. You will find the story in "The River that God Forgot" by Richard Collen. Your library is sure to have a copy.
Another change in the port was the change-over from sail to steam. Coal from the Lancashire coalfield was plentiful and transport by railway was easy. As a result the port prospered and other docks were built along the coastline. Find out who built most of the docks. He was a Yorkshireman and his story is to be found in **"Seaport"** by **Quentin Hughes** (Lund Humphries). The docks are still expanding today with the new container port at Seaforth. Trade in the nineteenth century increased. More and more people came to work and live in Liverpool. Where did they all come from?

Liverpool at the end of the 18th cent.

A4. Welcome stranger

A city like Liverpool which faces the sea must expect visitors and during the nineteenth century they poured into the town. It has been estimated that in 1851 out of all the adults in the town, less than one quarter had been born there.
The Welsh had for long come to Merseyside to trade. By 1787 sufficient numbers of them had stayed to found and build the Welsh Methodist Chapel in Pall Mall. In 1793, the Bishop of Chester gave permission for services in St. Paul's Church to be performed in Welsh. Then in 1840 that most Welsh of festivals, the **Eisteddfod,** was held in Liverpool.
Among the Welsh who came was a Mr. Owen. He set up shop in Liverpool and did much to change the shopping habits of the land. Most of the selling a hundred years ago was carried on by haggling at market stalls. Mr. Owen insisted on one price and no arguments. This gentleman started a shopping revolution and greatly expanded. His store still flourishes in the centre of Liverpool.
Many of the houses which were built in the house-building boom of the nineteenth century were constructed by Welshmen.
Two Welsh builders of this time have left their mark in Liverpool in an unusual way. The streets from Spellow Lane in Walton going North are:— Oxton, Winslow, Eton, Neston, Andrew, Nimrod, Dane, Wilburn, Ismay, Lind, Lowell, Index, Arnot, Makin, Olney, Weldon, Euston, Nixon. When the first letters of each street are put together they read:—Owen and William Owen, the names of the two Welsh brothers who were contractors and who built the houses there.
The streets around your home or school may have something in common. Some streets in a neighbourhood are named after flowers, some like the ones in the Dingle are named after Biblical characters, which accounts for the local people calling the area "The Holy Land"!
What can you find out about the street names in your area?

The Irish

Many Welshmen arrived but a far greater number came to Liverpool from Ireland. When the potato crop failed in 1845, the Irish people faced starvation. They had depended on potatoes as their main food. To survive, they left their homes in their thousands. In the first three months of 1847, 144 000 Irish landed at Liverpool and only 16 000 managed to get ships to America. Many were forced to stay in Liverpool either waiting for a boat or trying to find work.
There was not enough housing. 27 128 people were living in cellars in terrible conditions. There was no means of getting rid of refuse. Many of the cellars were so small a man could not stand upright. Some had no windows and yet others had cesspools beneath the floor.
Most of the Irish were desperately poor and could only afford the cheapest lodging. The charge for a night in one of these dark cellars was a penny a person.

Disease was rampant. It took the hard work of **Doctor Duncan** (1805–1863), Liverpool's first Medical Officer of Health, to get the situation under control.
Some of the Irish never reached America. They stayed in Liverpool living in these hovels near the centre of the town. They formed one of the main sources of casual labour for the docks. Others moved out to the coalfield of South-West Lancashire and settled in places like St. Helens.
As the port grew many people from distant lands became citizens of Liverpool. Liverpool was their first port after leaving their homelands. The longer they stayed, the more they felt at home here. Many could not afford to return over the seas, even if they had wanted to.

Dr. Duncan.

More recent newcomers

A large number of Chinese came. They were industrious and soon set up Chinese laundries and later restaurants. They brought with them their customs, their language and unusual recipes.
Visit a Chinese restaurant and look closely at the menu. What ingredients are used? Make a list of all the foods served in a Chinese restaurant which you do not normally eat at home.
Another group, the West Indians, left their islands and the sun to come to England full of hope for a better life.
During the twentieth century, Indians and Greeks have settled in Liverpool. They, like the Chinese, have been largely employed in keeping restaurants and fish and chip shops supplying food and recipes from their homeland for the people of Liverpool.
When, at the beginning of the twentieth century, the Jews were forced to leave their homelands in Central Europe and Russia, they set off on their travels. Many came to Liverpool on their way to America and never completed the journey, for they settled in the port. The Jewish Board of Guardians in Liverpool looked after the Jewish poor.
The people from abroad continue to arrive on Merseyside. Africans from Nigeria and Ghana are joining all the other visitors who have now become part of the community.
The surnames of people tell us something about our ancestors. Make a list of the surnames in your class, noting where you think the surnames originated.

Surnames were not very common in the past. In 1379 out of 86 people who paid poll tax in Liverpool only 13 had surnames. Some surnames arose from places or jobs or even nicknames. They often described someone as "the son of another person". ("Ap" in Welsh, "ben" in Hebrew.)
We can find many names in the Merseyside telephone directory which tell us a little about the origins of some people—although many will have lost trace of where their ancestors came from:

13 pages of Jones from Wales
9 pages of Williams from Wales
6 pages of Roberts from Wales
5 pages of Hughes from Wales
21 pages of Mac's from Scotland and Ireland
9 pages of Smiths from England
2 pages of Murphys from Ireland
2 pages of Kellys from Ireland

The great majority of these would regard themselves as Liverpudlians.

A5. At the flick of a switch

Many things are taken for granted in today's homes on Merseyside; we can turn on the light, a tap will bring water and a gas fire will bring warmth. These luxuries would have amazed our ancestors.

Gas

Gas was used for lighting some streets in London in 1805, the year when Nelson won a naval victory at Trafalgar. It was not until 1815 that a company was formed to make and sell gas in Liverpool. A Mr. James Hargreaves, who had had some experience of the gas industry in London, came to Liverpool to start the undertaking. He made contact with Jonathan Varty, a coach maker of Dale Street. Mains were laid and a gas-making plant was erected in the cellar of Varty's premises. Varty's insurers, The Sun Life Company, became worried and threatened to withdraw his policy but the work proceeded and on the 26th of January 1816 The Liverpool Mercury reported in its columns.
"Two large gas lamps, with three burners in each have been lighted with gas and exhibited for the last few nights at the front of the Town Hall. The lighting is so brilliant that a person may with ease discover the hour by his watch at a distance of 20 or 30 yards".
A scale of charges was issued in 1816. The charges were based on the size of burners and the time they burned. The use of these burners from sunset to 8 p.m. cost two guineas (£2·10) per annum and £4·50 if the light remained burning until midnight. There were no gas meters in those days. The new lighting soon became fashionable. The Theatre Royal in Williamson Square was equipped in 1818 and the Royal Amphitheatre in 1826.
In 1819 a street lighting contract was signed and by the end of the year 229 lamps were in operation. It was not until 1850 that gas came to be used in private homes.

Electricity

By this time electricity had come upon the scene. In 1896 Bold Street was lit by a number of arc lamps but these were easily damaged and ordinary electric bulbs were not very powerful. In 1921 there were only 16 kilometres of streets lit by electricity. With the increase of cars on the roads and their greater speeds, there came the need to light the streets in a more efficient manner.
By 1937, 620 kilometres of streets were lit by electricity. Nowadays the figure is about 1610 kilometres of Liverpool's streets. In 1934 the **Amber Sodium** lights were tried out for the first time in the world in Liverpool. In 1953 the first cold cathode fluorescent lamps in the country were tried out at the Pier Head.
What kind of lighting does your street have? Find out when it was installed. The style of the lamp post should give you a clue.
The City took over the Liverpool Electric Supply Company in 1896, but the Merseyside and North Wales Electricity Board took it over in 1947.

Some Liverpool street lamps.

Water

The ease of turning on a tap or flushing a toilet is perhaps also taken very much for granted today and yet these systems are only about a hundred years old.
The water supply of the city in the mid-nineteenth century was very poor indeed. The sewers were very inefficient and the lack of water to flush the whole system was a serious problem. Samuel Holme, a local politician, wrote: *"I never hail anything with greater delight than I do a violent tempest or a terrific thunderstorm accompanied by heavy rain, for these are the scavengers that thousands have to cleanse away any impurities and the filth in which they live, or rather exist".*
Water came from wells which were inadequate and in 1846 the Corporation took over the supply of water and the sewage system in the Sanitary Act of 1846. After much debate a reservoir was constructed at Rivington near Chorley and by 1857 the Rivington Water Works were in full swing. By 1881 a scheme for bringing water from Lake Vyrnwy was begun. More and more water is needed today. Water comes from the following places:
Lake Vyrnwy—173 million litres daily; Rivington—23 million litres daily; Huntington—124 million litres daily; Deep wells at Green Lane and Dudlow Lane in Liverpool—4 543 000 litres every year.
In 1965 a new reservoir at **Llyn Celyn** was opened. The Llyn Celyn dam controls the flow of water in the River Dee. The water flows down the river until it reaches Huntington near Chester. At

Llyn Celyn.

Huntington it is taken out and taken by aqueduct to Liverpool. 320 million litres flow into Liverpool daily and 86 million litres a day are supplied to areas on the way to Liverpool. These vast quantities are needed because *each person* on average uses 290 litres per day and industry requires 91 000 litres each day in addition.
Make a list of all the ways you use water *every day* and make an approximate calculation of how much you personally need.

Sanitation

Water was the first need but sewers were essential. **Dr. Duncan,** whom you have already heard about was the first Medical Officer of Health for Liverpool and the first in Britain. He campaigned for an efficient sanitation system. He had seen the terrible overcrowding and filth in the cellars where some of the Irish lived and had been involved in treating victims of the cholera outbreak. He was responsible for bringing this terrible situation before the public. He was accused of being *"not nice"* but he used the statistics gathered in his work among the poor to bring about the Sanitation Act of 1846. One calculation he made was that the average age at death in Liverpool was nineteen. The Act was passed despite the opposition.
If you want to know more about the conditions during **Dr. Duncan's** day read *Redburn* by Herman Melville, an American writer who visited Liverpool and saw for himself how bad the situation was.

But Acts of Parliament do not change conditions over-night. In 1847 when the starving Irish came over in their thousands, typhus fever raged in the city. In Dr. Duncan's first year as Medical Officer of Health, 21 000 people died. Money was voted by the Council to build drains and sewers. **John Newlands** was the engineer who was responsible for the operation. In 1847 there were 85 km. of sewers. In 1857 another 129 km. had been added and a further 116 km of main sewers. Streets were paved and street sweepers kept them clean.

Progress in the Social Service

Merseyside has seen many examples of social services. Here are some; perhaps you can add some more.

First!

Liverpool had the first:

School for the Blind	1791
Public Baths and Wash houses	1842
Medical Officer of Health	1847
Provincial Children's Hospital	1851
District Nurse	1859
Provincial Nurses' School	1862
Society for the Prevention of Cruelty to Children	1883
School of Tropical Medicine	1899

Assignments for Theme A

Merseyside Now and Then

1. Things to discuss.

(i) Where did Liverpool obtain its wealth in the 18th and 19th centuries? Why did the city grow so rapidly? Why did so many people come here?

(ii) What have the people of different nationalities, cultures and races contributed to the life of Merseyside?

(iii) Why do you think many of the Liverpool merchants objected to the view of William Roscoe on slavery?

2. Things to do.

(i) Visit the Docks at Liverpool and Birkenhead and note the names of the ships and their home ports. Also note what cargoes are being loaded and unloaded. (Before you visit the Docks you must obtain a permit from the Mersey Docks and Harbour Company.)

(ii) When you have found out where the sandstone outcrops are on Merseyside, make a model to show a cross section of the ground beneath the surface around the estuary. Find pieces of actual sandstone to represent the outcrops.

(iii) Take a bus ride into Liverpool. Use a notebook to record the places which are obviously associated with people who have come to settle on Merseyside, like churches and restaurants.

3. Things to find out.

(i) Find out about the work of the Liverpool Community Relations Council. What does it aim to do? The Senior Community Relations Officer whose office is at 64 Mount Pleasant will be able to help you.

(ii) Where are the main power stations on Merseyside which supply the area with electricity?

(iii) Find out about the life of William Roscoe. You can see his statue in Sefton Park. What places in Liverpool have been named after him?

Theme B Transport on Merseyside

B1. Getting around

Look at an atlas showing the population density of the British Isles. You will see that Merseyside is one of the areas in the country where a great many people live per 2·5 square kilometres. If you look round your own school or home you should realise what *population density of more than 100 per 2·5 square kilometres* means. It means there are a great many people living on Merseyside, and that the area is almost completely built up. It means you can travel from the centre of Liverpool for a distance of at least 13 km in any direction without coming across a strip of countryside. On Merseyside, one town leads into another, and yet another. We call this an urban area, or **conurbation.** The population of this conurbation as you have

seen from the previous chapter is about two million people. Many of these people have to travel from home to work. This may mean travelling from home to work in the nearest urban centre to where they live. Many people make a daily journey to the centre of Liverpool from outlying towns. Liverpool is the centre of the conurbation. Liverpool is an important marketing, industrial and transport centre and it provides a wide range of professional and commercial services. The city also provides cultural, religious, and specialised educational and medical facilities. If you look at this map you will be able to pick out a continuous coloured line. A very large number of the people who live inside the area enclosed by this coloured line work in Liverpool. As you can see they have to travel a long way to work.

On this map you can also see an even bigger area enclosed by a black dotted line. Many of the people who live inside this line often go to Liverpool to visit the big shops. This is the area also which is served by Liverpool wholesalers who stock the local shops.

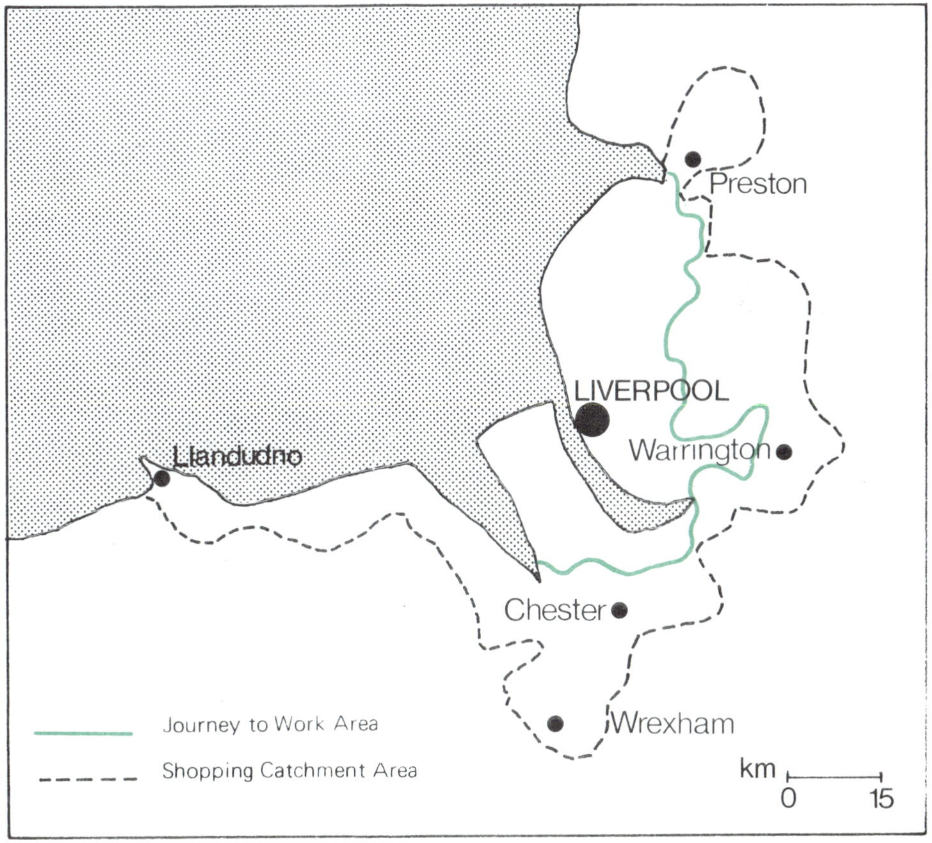

Transport system

What holds this vast conurbation together? What are the arteries along which the life-blood of Merseyside flows? They are of course the conurbation's transport system, its railways, roads, and ferries. Because Liverpool is a port, an efficient transport system is important to carry goods from the Docks to other parts of Britain. Liverpool lands 25 per cent, in terms of *value,* of the nation's trade.

Before you read about the various forms of transport on Merseyside here are some things for you to find out.

1. You know the population of Merseyside is about two million. Find out the size of the population of Tokyo, London, New Zealand, Iceland, Australia, Norway and Sri Lanka (Ceylon). Are these places in terms of population bigger or smaller than Merseyside?
2. If you want to compare the centre of a great city with your district look at a "25 in.:1 mile" map of the main street or road in the area. Fill in the map to show what the buildings are used for. You will have to devise a suitable key to show their various uses. Compare *your* map with an official map and pictures of central Liverpool.
3. If you want to know what the movement of people about a great city looks like, do a traffic survey at a local road junction early in the morning, at midday and at about 5.30 p.m.

Traffic congestion, as it used to look.

B2. Road transport

The Merseyside Passenger Transport Executive is the organisation responsible for providing public road transport in this area. It is in fact an amalgamation, formed in 1970, of the old Liverpool, Birkenhead, and Wallasey Corporation Transport Authorities. Every bus belonging to the M.P.T.E. carries a special symbol. The ferries which cross the Mersey also belong to the M.P.T.E. and they also display the same crest. The M.P.T.E. has about 1300 vehicles. In the year 1969–70, 285 million passengers were carried.

Look at this photograph.

1. Consider the changes that have occurred in Liverpool since the first photograph was taken in:
   (*a*) the size of the streets;
   (*b*) the material the streets and roads are made of;
   (*c*) the street sounds and smells.

Above: M.P.T.A. symbol.
Right: Lord St. in 1908.

You may like to write a description of a street scene as you imagine you are travelling along in an older tram.

Left: Laying tram lines in a Liverpool street.
Above and right: Some Liverpool trams.

Look at the table below which contains a great deal of information about the changing pattern of public road transport from 1938–1956.

1. When did trams cease to be important?
2. Make a graph to show the number of passengers carried between 1938 and 1956.

		1938/39	1953/54	1954/55	1955/56
Passengers	Tram	257 233 948	49 000 000	40 000 000	29,000,000
	Bus	33 736 332	345 000 000	348 000 000	351 000 000
Mileage	Tram	21 203 346	5 046 639	4 152 793	3 293 477
	Bus	4 579 389	32 051 575	34 372 457	37 188 532
Fares paid (£s)	Tram	1 463 818	676 782	556 092	423 136
	Bus	283 372	4 230 514	4 478 513	4 823 736
Running costs (£s)	Tram	1 233 537	898 084	734 411	588 442
	Bus	208 129	3 511 763	3 828 356	4 325 786
Fleet numbers	Tram	781	207	177	118
	Bus	174	929	967	1 038

KEY: Tram, Bus

Public transport figures 1938–56.

Out of town services

Besides these services there are the inter-town and inter-city routes served by Lancashire United, Hebble, St. Helens and Wigan Corporation bus services to name a few. On an even bigger scale the Ribble Motor Services Company connects Liverpool with the rest of the North-West and with big cities elsewhere in the country. The Crosville Motor Services Company has many routes on Merseyside and provides a regular service to North Wales.

Bus services are a well thought out means of moving people about a densely populated area. The photograph shows the bus terminal at the Liverpool Pier Head. Can you mark any other bus terminal on a map of Liverpool? What have they all got in common? What does the word terminal mean?

Pier Head bus terminal.

The parking problem

For those people who travel to Liverpool by car, parking places have to be found by the Corporation. The only way this can be done is by building multi-storey car parks away from the city centre, but within walking distance of the offices and shops. This is a photograph of one of these multi-storey car parks in the process of being built. Soon there will be many like these. Find out where these are planned to go up.

Some of the ideas that the planners are working on include an attempt to separate different types of traffic. At Runcorn New Town for example a 'Busway' has been introduced. This is a special road in a figure of eight which will serve the whole town. Along the 'Busway' fast buses will serve homes, shops and factories on their own roadway free from other traffic.

In the centre of the cities and towns the problem is to keep pedestrians and traffic separate while allowing both to move about freely. In Liverpool pedestrian precincts like St. John's in the Centre have grown up recently. Old parts of the City like Bold Street have been cleared of traffic. Williamson Square is another part of the City that has changed in this way. Can you find out what other streets are planned as pedestrian precincts in the future?

Ideas like these are dependent on the existence of wide new roads or motorways to bring traffic into and out of the City quickly, and on the availability of carefully planned parking facilities for vehicles in and around the City.

Left: The building of a multi-storey car park
Below left: Busway at Runcorn.
Below: Bold St. pedestrian precinct.

B3. Crossing the Mersey

Motorways

Motorway construction is well under way in the North-West. Even the furthest points of the Merseyside area will be within one hour's travelling time of Liverpool by 1976. This map shows the motorway that will be in existence by then. The M6 runs 15 miles to the East of Liverpool, the **M62** will continue from the **M6** and run North to Manchester over the Pennines to the East Coast at Hull. Two other motorways, the **M56** and the **M53,** will link the **M6** with Merseyside. These motorways will run through North Cheshire and the Wirral and will link up with the Second Mersey Tunnel between Wallasey and Liverpool. One of the tubes of this Second Tunnel called 'Kingsway' was opened in 1971 and the second will be opened by the mid-seventies. A third river-crossing south of the present tunnels is proposed for the future. It will form a link from the Wirral through Liverpool to Preston.

There is also talk of building a causeway called **The Dee Barrage Scheme** across the River Dee and if this comes about there could be a motorway link direct from Liverpool into North Wales.

If this scheme comes about what effect do you think it will have on Merseyside? Will Merseyside start extending into North Wales and spread its area even further?

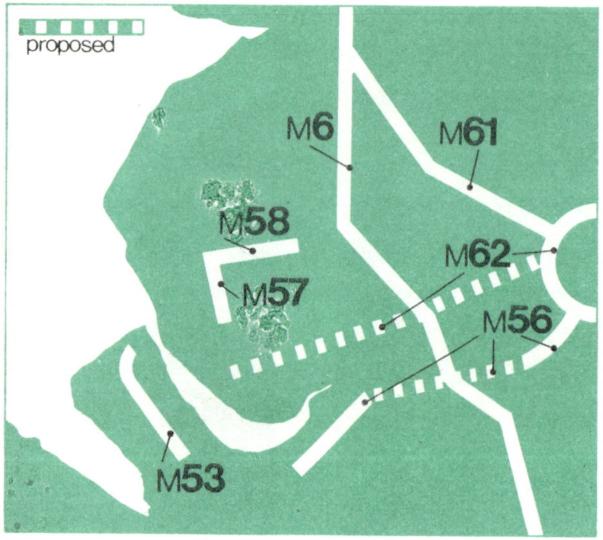

Motorways serving Merseyside.

The lowest bridging point on the River Mersey is the narrow gap between Widnes and Runcorn. This has been a fairly important river crossing site from earliest times. Up until the middle of the last century people used to cross the River Mersey at this point by ferry or sometimes by walking or riding on horseback across the sandbanks at low tide.

In 1868 the Runcorn "gap" was bridged by a railway bridge. This bridge completed a railway link between the Lancashire coalfields in mid-Cheshire and between Liverpool and the South. This photograph taken in 1960 shows the railway bridge but it also shows the new road bridge and the old "transporter". The transporter was a very rare type of bridge. It consisted of a platform suspended from steel cables which was drawn to and fro across the river, carrying a small load, by fixed engines on the bank.

The Widnes-Runcorn Transporter was opened in May 1905 and was closed in July 1961. A stone slab marks the place on the Widnes side where the Transporter used to start from. There was no longer any need for the Transporter when the new road bridge was opened in July 1961.

Look at the photograph again and consider what advantages the new road bridge has over the transporter. Why do you think a road bridge like this was not built sooner? Look at the Ordnance Survey Sheet 100. How do you think the construction of a road bridge has already affected the pattern of road building in the area? While you are looking at this map you can also get

Three bridges over the Mersey at Runcorn.

some idea of why there is no other bridge across the Mersey below Widnes and why the problem of crossing the river between Liverpool and the Wirral has been solved by using ferries or by tunnels under it.

Right: The 'Royal Iris' after the Zeebrugge raid.
Middle: A ferry boat at the Pier Head.
Far right: The Kingsway Tunnel.

Ferries

Ferries have been crossing the Mersey for many hundreds of years. Probably the earliest record of ferries operating here is The Crown Charter granted to the **Benedictine Priory** at Birkenhead in 1330. The early ferries were in the control of monks and they used to carry passengers across in small single-masted sailing boats. Ferries grew in number after the introduction of steam-powered boats. The first steam ferry was called 'The Etna' which started operating in 1817. Why do you think this early steam ferry was called 'The Etna'?

As the population of the Wirral expanded, the number of ferries increased and by 1840 ferries were operating from New Brighton, Egremont, Seacombe, Woodside, Monks, Birkenhead, Tranmere, Rock Ferry, New Ferry and Eastham. Find out which of these ferries are still operating. Also find out where the 1840 landing places were and mark them on a map.

The best known of the ferry boats on the Mersey were probably the "Daffodil" and the "Iris".

During the First World War these ferries were renamed "The Royal Daffodil" and "The Royal Iris" for the part they played in the commando raid on Zeebrugge on St. George's Day 1918. These two ferry boats belong to a long line of "Flower Boats" built in the late nineteenth and early twentieth centuries like "Waterlily", "Wildrose", "Mayflower", "Heatherbell", "Daisy", "Primrose", "Crocus" and "Snowdrop".
Go on a visit to the River Mersey at the Pier Head and ride on the ferry.

Under the Mersey

When people talk about the Mersey Tunnel they are usually talking about the road tunnel opened in 1934. It is called Queensway as opposed to the new tunnel opened in 1971 called Kingsway. In its first year Queensway was used by $2\frac{3}{4}$ million vehicles. By 1968 the number of vehicles using the tunnel was 19 million which was why the second tunnel was built.
The first tunnel under the Mersey, however, was for a railway line opened in 1886 between Liverpool (James Street) and Birkenhead (Green Lane). In "The Times" the progress of the excavation was reported each week. On Tuesday, 8th January, 1884, it reported:
"Operations of these works during the past week have exceeded all previous efforts, the distance advanced under the river being no less than 46 yards, of which 33 yards were done by Beaumont's boring machine on the Birkenhead side. The distance to be excavated is now less than 60 yards, and it is expected that the passage under the Mersey will be completed next week.
The men working on the heading on one side can now hear the sound of their colleagues working in the opposite heading".
By 1892 this line had been extended to Rock Ferry and Liverpool Central. At first this railway line was not successful as the steam locomotives created unbearable smoke and soot in the underground stations and tunnels.
In 1903 electric trains were introduced solving the problem and by 1905 the number of people crossing the River by train overtook the numbers using the ferry.

B4. Railways

The electrification of the Mersey Railway was copied by the Liverpool and Southport line in 1904 and the Wirral lines in the 1930's. These lines played an important part in the development of modern Liverpool providing transport for commuters and making possible the growth of Liverpool's suburbs. On the Wirral, Wallasey, West Kirby, New Brighton and Hoylake became dormitory towns for Liverpool businessmen. On similar lines on the Liverpool side Crosby and Southport grew in size.

One of Liverpool's most famous railways was **'The Overhead'** that ran the length of Dockland from Dingle to Bootle. This railway was intended to transport the dockers from one dock to another. Built in 1893 it was the first elevated electrically-operated railway in the world. It was called the "Dockers' Umbrella" by Liverpool people. Why do you think it was called this? It is now no more. It was dismantled in 1956 because it had become too expensive to repair. You can learn a great deal about this railway

Left: An electric train at Wallasey.
Above: An advertisement for the Overhead Railway.
Right: The Overhead Railway.

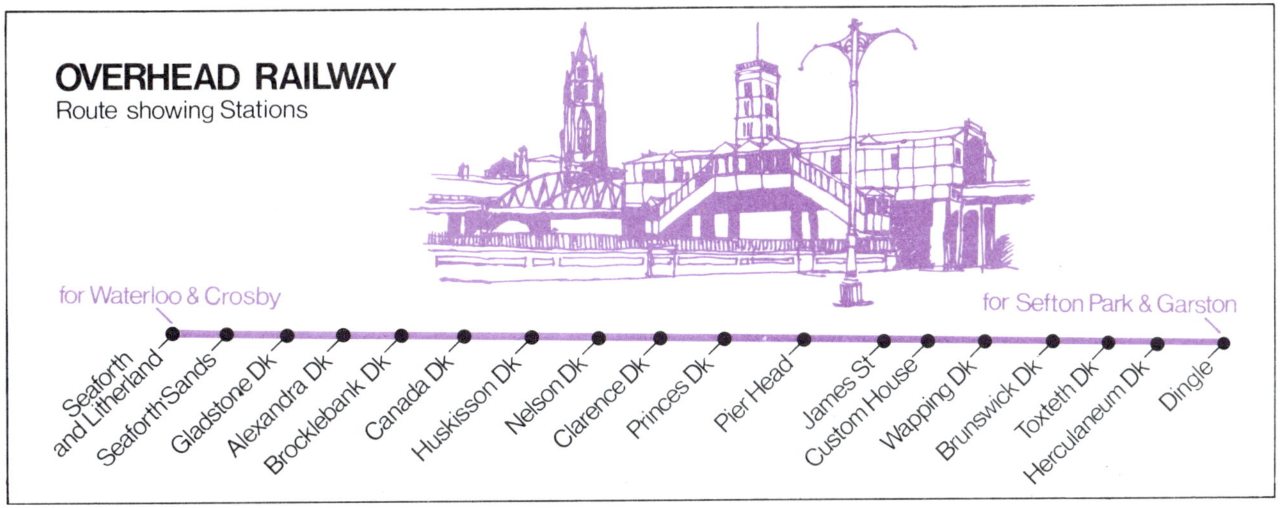
OVERHEAD RAILWAY
Route showing Stations
for Waterloo & Crosby
for Sefton Park & Garston
Seaforth and Litherland
Seaforth Sands
Gladstone Dk
Alexandra Dk
Brocklebank Dk
Canada Dk
Huskisson Dk
Nelson Dk
Clarence Dk
Princes Dk
Pier Head
James St
Custom House
Wapping Dk
Brunswick Dk
Toxteth Dk
Herculaneum Dk
Dingle

by visiting the Liverpool City Museum.
The modern City plans for the efficient movement of people into and out of the City include the Mersey Railway Terminal Loop. The plan is that the trains from the Wirral will go round the City Centre underground, serving underground stations at James Street, Moorfields, Lime Street, Central Station and returning to James Street again. There *may* also be a Southport, Ormskirk, Gateacre, Warrington Line connecting with the terminal loop at Moorfields and Central Stations. What advantages will an underground circling the City Centre bring? Who will use it? Will it lead to less congestion in the streets of Liverpool?
If you look at this diagram you will realise how extensive the suburban and local rail facilities are and help to keep Merseyside as one unit. The Wirral Line is the busiest suburban line in England outside London. Here are some things for you to do:

1. Compare the Mersey rail diagram with Ordnance Survey Sheet 100.
2. Collect timetables for the services operating on Mersey rail:
   (*a*) Draw a diagram showing how long each journey takes.
   (*b*) Find out which areas have the frequent services.
3. Why are parking facilities provided at some Mersey rail stations?

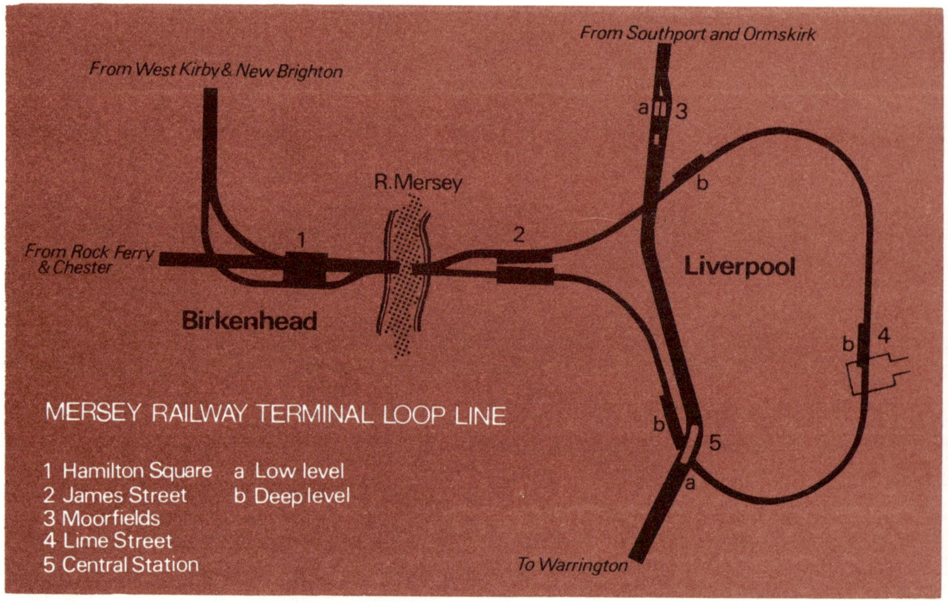

The Overhead Railway in 1908.

The birth of the railway age

Liverpool was in fact the birthplace of the railway. The Liverpool and Manchester Railway you have already read about was opened in September 1830. It was the first passenger-carrying railway in the world.
On the opening day many famous figures joined the other passengers on the journey from Liverpool to Manchester. The event was watched by thousands of people. This was the start of the railway era that heralded a modern age in Europe, pioneered the American West and made possible the conquest and the opening up of vast continents like Australia, India and Africa.
Unfortunately, the opening day was marred by the fatal injury to **William Huskisson,** M.P., at Parkside, near Newton-le-Willows where the trains had stopped. Huskisson had got out of his carriage to shake hands with the Duke of Wellington who was the Prime Minister at the time. He was struck by the "Rocket" and had his leg badly crushed. He died in Eccles and was buried in Liverpool.

Statue of William Huskisson.

The Steam Engines which competed for the prize of £500 offered by the Liverpool & Manchester Railway Co., 1829

1. Find out about Huskisson and his work. His name has been given to many places in Liverpool. Find out where these are.
2. At the time of the opening of the Liverpool to Manchester Railway, there was much opposition from the landowners and the canal operators. Why do you think they objected? Find out all you can about what people felt at the time about the new "Railway Age".
3. The construction of this railway was a great feat of engineering. It involved cutting miles of rock, laying an iron road across the quaking peat bog of Chat Moss, building a nine-arch viaduct over the valley of Sankey Brook and erecting 63 bridges between Liverpool and Manchester. Follow the railway on an Ordnance Survey map from Liverpool to Manchester. Find out as much as you can about the "Rainhill Trials" and the engines that competed there.

Inter City

Since that day Liverpool and Merseyside have been well served with railway connections. Important developments of recent times are the electrification of the Liverpool, London (Euston) main line in 1965 and the opening of the freight terminal in Garston. The Garston terminal handles 741 984 tonnes every year. The electrified line puts Liverpool in very fast contact with London and the Midlands. Among the vast amount of important freight it carries are the daily trains from Fords Halewood to Fords Dagenham.
The British Rail poster "The Liverpool Overground" illustrates Merseyside's rail connections with the rest of the country and also gives travelling times.

Below: Overhead electrification, main line Liverpool to London.
Right: British Rail Poster.

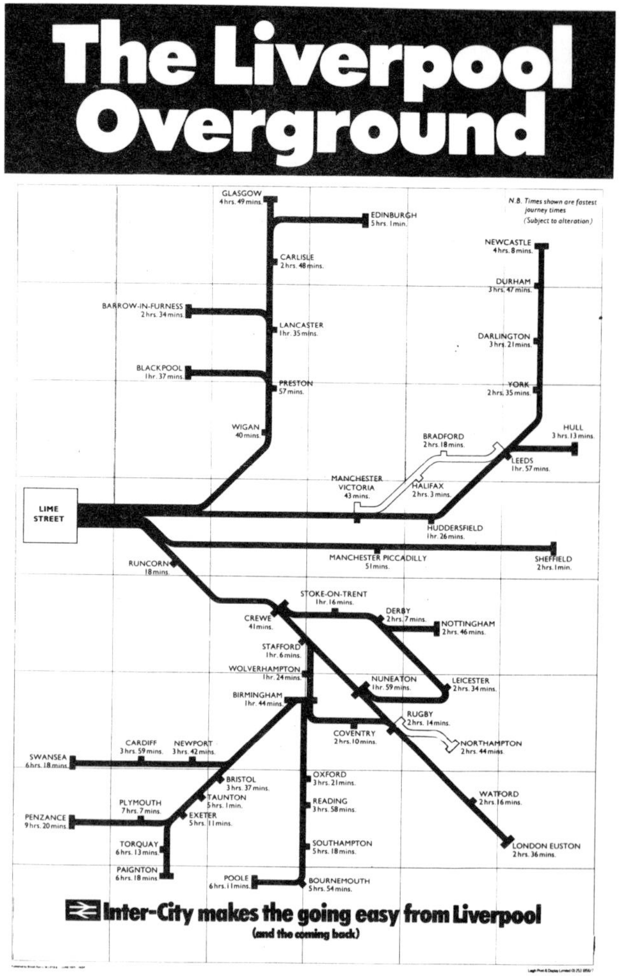

B5. Liverpool Airport

Liverpool Airport is situated on the banks of the River Mersey 13 km from the centre of the City at Speke. Speke is famous for its historical Tudor house called Speke Hall. In more recent times a large housing estate has been built in Speke. The Airport was officially opened on 1st July 1933 by the Marquis of Londonderry. On 3rd July, two days after the opening an advertisement appeared announcing regular services from Speke to Blackpool and the Isle of Man. Shortly afterwards the Dutch Airline K.L.M. opened up air routes between Liverpool and places like Amsterdam, Rotterdam and Malmo. By 1939 a modern air-terminal building had been finished which is the one you will see today if you visit the Airport for yourself.

Before the Second World War not many people travelled by air but since then the number of flights to and from Speke Airport has steadily increased.

This increase has resulted in a constant need to extend the runways to accommodate the faster airliners which came into service with the increase in the use of jet power.

Recently the City of Liverpool which owns the airport, invested £3 million in the construction of a new runway. Nearly 2000 tonnes of steel reinforcement has gone into this new runway which is equal to a normal 34 kilometre roadway in area. It is 2250 metres in length and is well capable of handling the large airliners of the present day. The surface is specially drained to prevent airliners aquaplaning or skidding. It is one of the safest in Britain. The runway was officially declared open on 19th September 1969.

A further 10 million pounds is to be spent on making Speke into an *international* airport.

Compare this diagram with a 6″ Ordnance Survey Map of the area (SJ 48 SW) and identify some of the roads and buildings surrounding the airport.

Liverpool Airport: Runways.

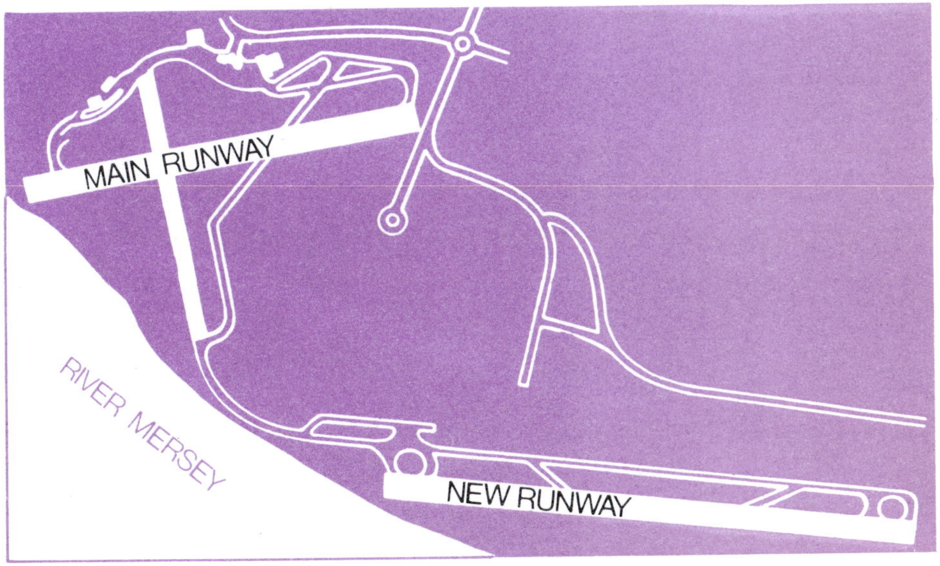

DAN-AIR LONDON

	Air Transport Movements						Passengers				Freight
								TERMINAL			
	TOTAL	Schedule	Charter	Private & Executive	Aero club	Others	TOTAL	Schedule	Charter	Transit	Metric Tons
1951	19 507	5 444	797	683	8 818	3 765	83 942	77 005	4 141	2 796	1 322
1954	18 337	5 184	598	890	8 810	2 855	102 554	85 711	13 267	3 576	902
1958	15 249	6 764	792	1 368	4 658	1 667	136 681	110 914	20 250	5 517	581
1962	18 790	11 427	1 383	3 018	574	2 388	292 973	235 963	27 512	29 498	3 292
1966	34 715	17 346	2 309	3 692	8 105	3 263	479 806	406 254	44 590	28 962	16 681
1970	54 349	15 303	*	*	*	*	441 341	*	*	*	19 912

*Figures not available

	I.O.M IN	I.O.M OUT	Belfast IN	Belfast OUT	Manches/r IN	Manches/r OUT	London IN	London OUT	Newcastle IN	Newcastle OUT	Cardiff IN	Cardiff OUT	Bristol IN	Bristol OUT	Glasgow IN	Glasgow OUT	Stansted IN	Stansted OUT	Leeds IN	Leeds OUT	Norwich IN	Norwich OUT	Others
JAN	2625	2063	2257	1473	23	41	2914	3 430	71	67	381	396	299	335	1038	1084	34	19	34	35			70
FEB	2 305	2174	1706	1406	3	69	3031	3359	108	88	439	337	347	322	1084	1185			5	7			64
MAR	2 851	2885	1756	1 649	6	11	4 303	4703	127	125	386	379	395	339	1202	1 307	365	365	9	5			59
APR	4485	4427	1597	1697			4951	5 111	119	111	454	296	421	293	1271	1 353			155	149			24
MAY	4536	5 753	1300	1504		6	5 068	5 152	82	89	637	425	538	326	1368	1516			4	4			348
JUN	7307	6 807	1571	1 545	4		5 000	4 954	154	102	546	356	670	344	1473	1611	7		3	2			29
JUL	6030	6 470	1 871	2 433			5170	5473	153	117	622	425	607	434	1518	1 649					40	40	50
AUG	7798	7 111	2028	2 139			4779	5140	104	90	649	405	658	346	1273	1489					12	14	24
SEP.	6635	5 246	1695	1 590			5 021	5411	100	93	566	459	669	402	1461	1 676					19	15	56
OCT	4306	3950	1377	1440	1	4	4774	5083	168	151	367	347	441	289	1 348	1 538		1			21	24	167
NOV																							
DEC																							

Liverpool Airport: Transport details.

Ask yourself the question whether the increased use of the airport poses a threat to anyone or anything.

Every passenger who passes through the airport is counted and at the end of every month a total is calculated of the passenger movement to and from Liverpool to various parts of Britain and abroad. This table gives the yearly figures from 1951 onwards. Make graphs to show the number of aeroplanes and passengers using the airport between 1951 and 1966.

Can you find figures more recent than these?

Make a histogram (block graph) to show the different categories of flights using the airport in 1966.

Compare the amount of freight handled by Liverpool Airport with the amount handled by the Mersey Docks and Harbour Company and British Rail in Liverpool.

Look at this table and mark all these airports on a map of the British Isles. As a class exercise you can work out the total number of passengers brought into Liverpool by air from each airport and display this diagrammatically as a histogram. Do the same for passengers flying out of Liverpool.

Left: Liverpool Airport.

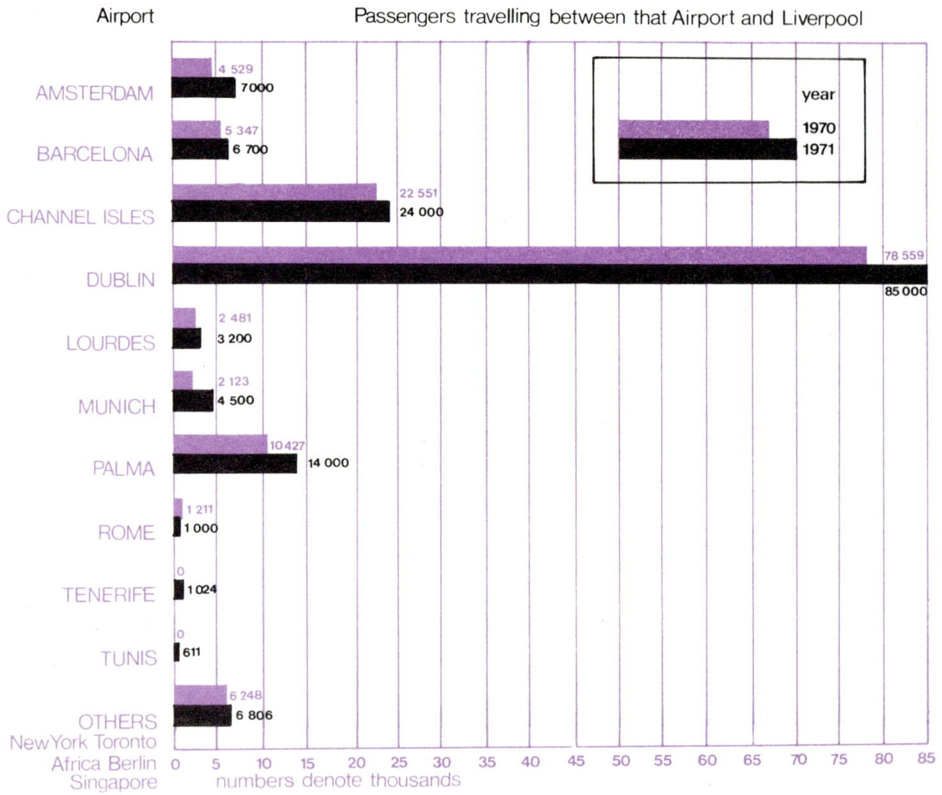

Above: Freight being loaded into a Boeing 737.
Right: Liverpool Airport: Passenger details.

This third table shows how many passengers fly abroad from Liverpool. The table gives the figures for 1970 and 1971. Mark all the overseas airports that share traffic with Liverpool on a World map first and then on a map of Europe and North Africa.

Draw a histogram for 1970 and one for 1971, to show variations in passenger traffic like the one you worked out for domestic flights. Why do you think some airports are more popular than others? You might like to discuss with your teacher the reasons people have for travelling to various airports.

Assignments for Theme B

Transport on Merseyside

1. Things to discuss.

(i) Why do people living in the outlying parts of Merseyside travel into Liverpool?
(ii) How does "high density housing" affect your life?
(iii) What effect will the plan for improving the traffic-flow around Liverpool have on business men, shoppers, and casual visitors?

2. Things to do.

(i) Take a trip on a ferry to Birkenhead or Seacombe. Note all the different kinds of ships you can see in the River. Take a tape-recorder with you and record the sounds of the river. A camera is also essential to capture the sights you can see, especially the sky line.
(ii) When you return from your trip back on the ferry make a frieze of the various buildings which stand out. Pay particular attention to details like the names of firms you see on the waterfront.
(iii) Make a model of a ferry-boat showing how the passengers embark and disembark.
(iv) Make a model showing the hazards which the engineers who built the Liverpool and Manchester Railway had to overcome. To sense the atmosphere visit Edge Hill Station, where the first of all railways had its terminus.
(v) Visit Liverpool Airport. Note all the airliners which use Speke and where they are bound for. You will see the arrivals and departures shown on a television screen just inside the door.

3. Things to find out.

(i) Find out how many cars used each of the Mersey tunnels last year.
(ii) What plans are there in your area to set up traffic-free pedestrian areas?
(iii) Find out how long it takes to cross the Mersey:
(*a*) by ferry,
(*b*) by bus,
(*c*) by train.
(iv) Find out all you can about the Liverpool Overhead Railway. The Reference Department of the Picton Library will be able to help you with photographs and timetables. There are one or two parts of the old stations still in existence around the Dingle. Find out where these are and visit the places to try and reconstruct what a trip on the "Overhead" was like.

Theme C
Living on Merseyside

C1. Where they used to live

In the nineteenth century Liverpool housing was either very good or very bad. The rich, who made their fortunes as bankers, merchants or business men, lived in large well-built houses. These were not far from the city centre where those wealthy men conducted their businesses.
Near to Liverpool, at Everton, **Thomas Shaw,** a rich landowner, built a long line of fashionable terraced houses. He called the street after himself. You can see that the houses in Shaw Street were once very grand. Thomas Shaw rented or sold the houses to rich Liverpool business men. To attract them he provided each house with decorations which only the rich could afford. Each house had an iron balcony, an iron boot-scraper and fine iron railings. The doors were large and were supported by large columns. At the back there were stables for carriages and horses. Inside, the rooms were large and everywhere there were expensive decorations and furniture.
Here is a list of some of the people who lived in Shaw Street in 1868. What kind of people do you imagine them to have been?

SHAW-STREET

1 Aked Robert, merchant
3 Bew Thomas C. plasterer and builder
11 Aungier Mark, cattle salesman
35 Lodge Robt. Thos. M.D. and surgeon
(*Church-street Soho*
19 Cooper James R. ironmonger
43 Lockett John, wine merchant
47 Preston Edmund, shipowner
51 Roberts Robert, tea merchant
(*William Henry-street*
53 Cornforth Joseph, master mariner
77 Lane John, brewer
115 Shelmerdine, Thomas, architect
2 Leigh Peter, surgeon
10 Webster James, cotton broker
12 Conor Rev. John R., A. M. & Surrowgate
Baptist Chapel
(*College-street South*

"The Gentle Folk"

Some of the wealthy business men were called "carriage folk". This was because they were wealthy enough to build houses out in the country. To travel into town they would come by horse-drawn or railway carriage.
Some business men even moved across the Mersey to the quiet countryside of the Wirral as Liverpool expanded as a busy, noisy port.

Shaw Street.

The poor cry out

But for the poor it was a different story. Thousands were Irish, who had come to Liverpool to escape famine in 1846. They lived in squalid, cramped conditions.
The landowners wanted to make as much use of their land as possible and built enclosed courts to house the poor families. They built these courts close to one another. Here is a description of a "court" from **"Her Benny"** a novel written at this time by **Silas K. Hocking** which captures what living conditions were like.

"On the western side of Scotland Road—that is to say, between it and the docks—there is a regular network of streets, inhabited by the lowest classes of the Liverpool poor. And those who have occasion to penetrate their dark and filthy recesses are generally thankful when they find themselves safe out again. In the winter these streets and courts are kept comparatively clean by the heavy rains; but in the summer the air fairly reeks with the stench of decayed fish, rotting vegetables, and every other conceivable kind of filth".

A Doctor working in Spencer Court said it had a smell "bad enough to raise the roof off his head".
Inside the court the picture was just as depressing. Here is another passage from "Her Benny".
"The furniture consisted of a three-legged round table, a chair minus a leg, and a three-legged stool. On the window-sill stood a glass bottle with a candle stuck in the neck, and under the stairs there was a heap of rags and shavings on which Benny and his sister slept".
The room described here would have been about three metres square. Measure this space out on the classroom floor.
In 1840 there were 2400 courts in which 86000 people lived. 38 000 people lived in cellars. You might also like to read "Her Benny" all through: it is very sad in parts. It gives you a clear idea of what it was like for a small boy growing up in terrible conditions.

Living conditions in a court in the 1930's.

Dr. Duncan to the rescue

Something had to be done to improve housing and get rid of disease which these conditions caused. You have already heard what Dr. Duncan did to put matters right. The courts were demolished and the Town Council set about building houses for the poor. In 1869 St. Martin's Cottages were built. 124 families were each housed in flats which had two or three bedrooms, a living room and a scullery. There was no bathroom, but there were washrooms and toilets on the landings. The people who moved there must have found them very different from their dark courts and cellars.

Soon other new tenements took shape. Victoria Square, built in the 1880's even had its own block of shops. This must have been one of the country's first shopping precincts.

By 1916 the redevelopment scheme to rehouse people had resulted in 2895 tenements and new dwellings being built.

Many tenement flats were built between the two world wars from 1919 to 1939. They were great lines or rings of flats often called "Gardens", but there were few flowers or trees to be seen.

St. Martin's Cottages.

Victoria Square.

The War

Liverpool was one of the chief targets for Nazi bombers during the 1939–1945 war. The bombs destroyed not only the docks and parts of the city centre but also many private homes. 4100 civilians were killed between 1940 and the 17th May 1942, during the blitz. 6585 houses were destroyed and 125 310 were damaged. Therefore, as soon as the war was over, a new programme of rebuilding was needed. Many families needed new homes because they had been "bombed out". And all those who lived in the "slums" also needed new homes.

Bombed houses in Liverpool.

Liverpool builds again

And so the bomb sites were quickly filled with specially-built prefabricated buildings. These were not made of bricks and mortar. Their walls and roofs were made in factories and bolted together on the site. These bungalows were designed to last for ten years. They were a temporary measure to house the many families who had been bombed out of their homes. Whole estates were erected and in all 3502 'pre-fabs', as they were called, were grouped around the city. Now few exist.

The long lines of old dwellings were overcrowded. Land for building new houses was desperately needed. Space was scarce in a built-up area like Liverpool. A new idea was thought of—building upwards so that many dwellings could be built on a small area of land. More redevelopment began.

The old houses had been built around narrow cobbled roads. These roads could not cope with the tremendous increase in the volume of traffic after the war. Modern wide roads now sweep through the city cutting clean lines through the older parts. This has been another reason for knocking down old property.

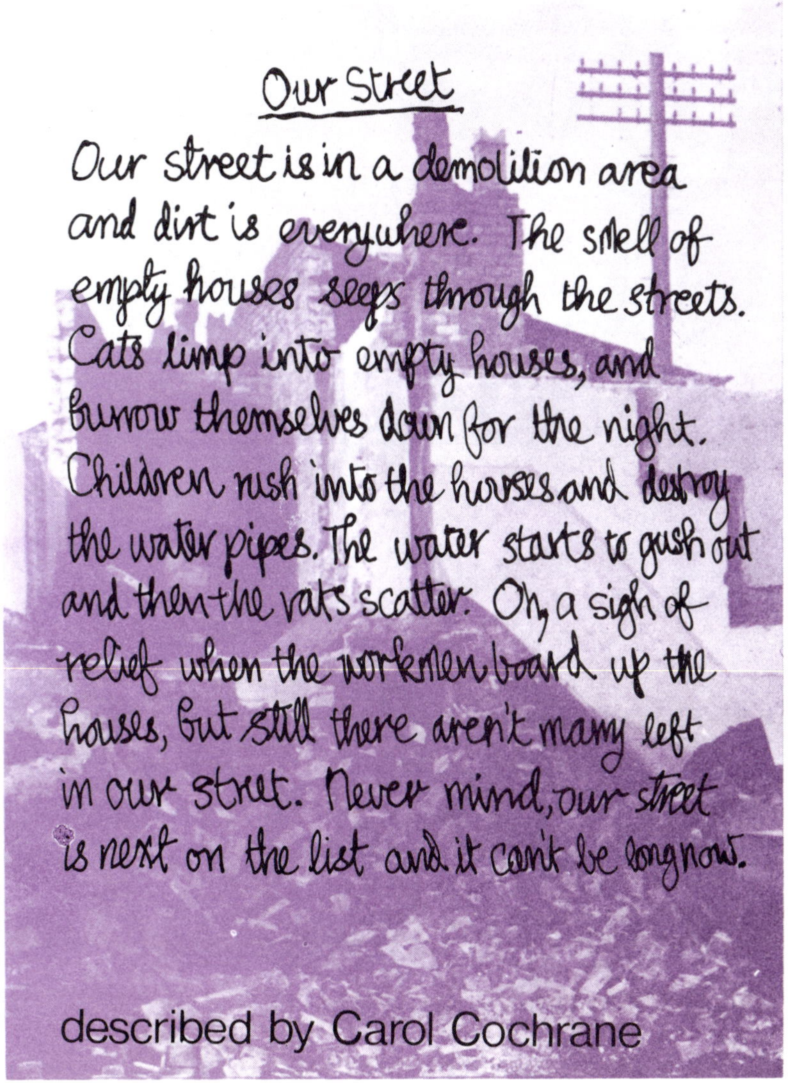

All this redevelopment has been necessary to provide better places for people to live in. When you knock houses down you often have to move families away from the area they grew up in. Redevelopment therefore is regarded with mixed feelings by those who are affected by it. Here is a description by a 14 yr. old Liverpool schoolgirl who knows what it is to live in a changing city.

Bottom left: A prefab near the end of its days.
Top left and left: High-rise flats.

C2. Moving out

Another answer to the problem of overcrowding in the city area was to build new estates and towns in the suburbs.

Before the Second World War, many people were moved from the heart of Liverpool to Norris Green, Walton, Clubmoor, Pinehurst Road, Dovecot and Huyton Farm. All these were outside the city centre, in places where land for building was available.

Between 1919 and 1939, 38 146 dwellings were built. This meant that over 100 000 people had new houses in those 20 years.

The new estates were called *Garden Cities*. Each house had a garden at the front and the back. Some streets were lined with trees and had open green spaces. They also had their own shopping centres within easy walking distance from all the houses.

Other housing estates were built further out from the city area, at Speke, Aintree and Kirkby. Houses were built alongside modern industrial estates so that workers would not have to travel far to work from their homes. Schools and shops were built on the estates.

At first, communities like **Speke** and **Kirkby** went through difficult times. There were not enough shops to supply the needs of the people. Converted vans, called mobile shops, roamed the streets selling food and household goods. Entertainment, especially for young people, was difficult to find. The cinemas and theatres were in Liverpool, a good hour's bus ride away.

Kirkby did much to improve facilities. Community centres and youth clubs were built so that people could meet, find recreation and talk about problems.

Left: Queens Drive housing estate.
Above: Housing estate at Kirkby.

Kirkby has grown to have its own athletics and sports stadium, swimming baths, civic centre, open air market, and a dozen youth clubs. Today places like Kirkby are townships in their own right.

Across the Mersey

In the 1930's many Liverpool families moved across the Mersey to the Wirral. They looked for employment in the carefully planned township of **Ellesmere Port** where homes and industry grew up together. They moved a few at a time as houses were completed. They were only allowed to settle there if they had a job in Ellesmere Port. These population figures show you how Ellesmere Port "boomed";—

1911	the population was	10 366
1931	the population was	18 911
1971	the population was	61 556

Planning and control are very important features of new towns. Once Ellesmere Port had been a small agricultural village. It grew into a prosperous industrial new town between the two World Wars. Today its modern factories turn out cars, paper, oil, and a host of manufactured goods.

Today's new towns

In the 1960's two new towns have attracted people away from Liverpool. **Skelmersdale** was once an agricultural area. Most of the people worked on the land or in the nearby coal mines. Many people became unemployed when the mines, like those of the White Moss Colliery, closed down.

Views of Skelmersdale New Town.

The other new town is **Runcorn.** Like Liverpool, Runcorn depended on imports for its livelihood. Its industries were based upon the processing of these imports. As ships grew larger they could not reach Runcorn. The Manchester Ship Canal attracted some industries, particularly I.C.I., to its banks. But more variety was needed, for about half the population of Runcorn depended on the chemical industry for work.

In Skelmersdale and Runcorn a new lease of life was needed—a shot in the arm to bring new growth and vigour. This came when they both were "designated" as New Towns, when new houses and new industry were harnessed together.

Shopping City, Runcorn New Town.

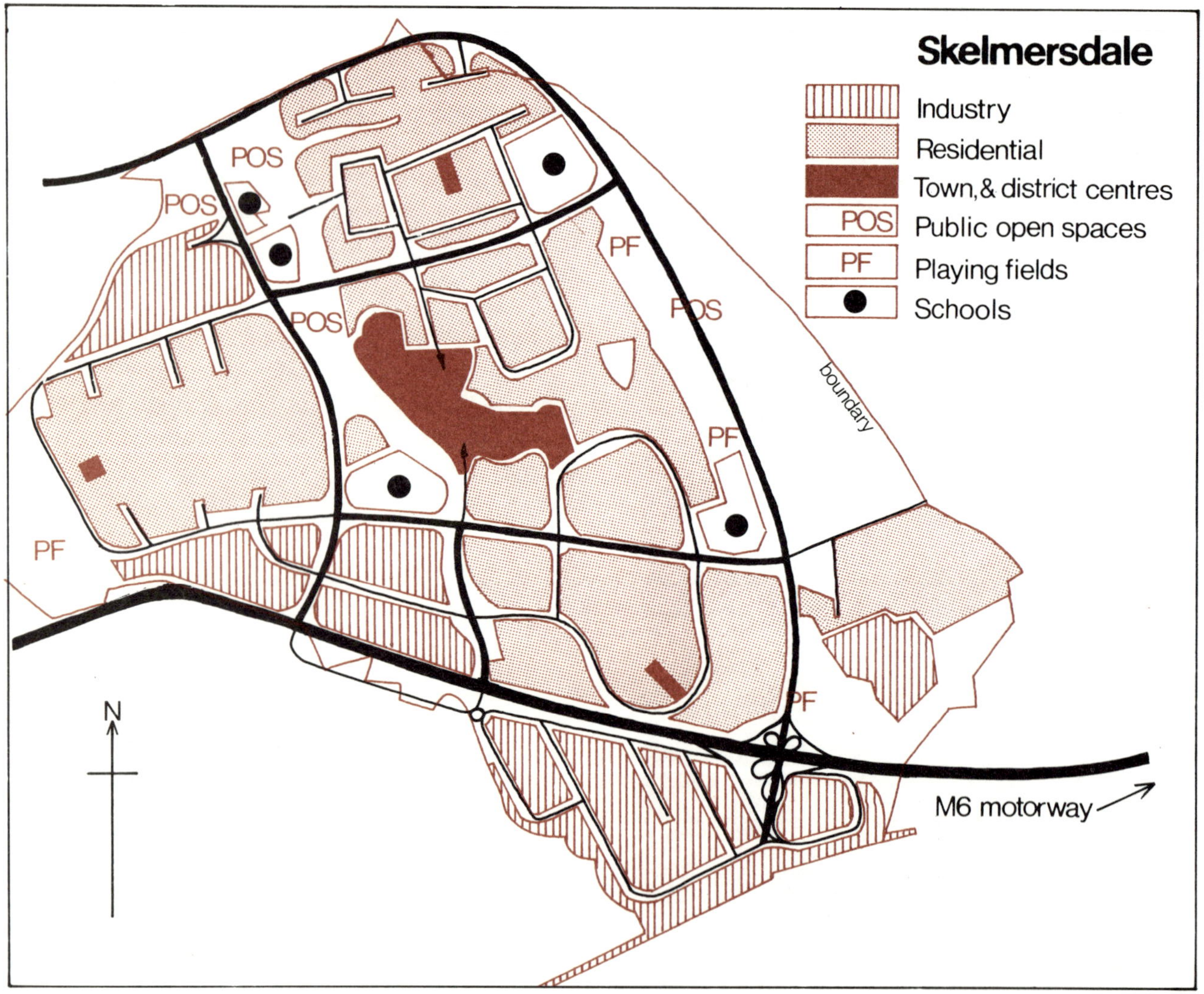

The maps of these towns show how factories and houses have been separated into estates, but they are close enough to be convenient for travelling. The houses are clean and bright. New towns are smokeless areas so that no smoke pollutes the air. The houses are centrally-heated. Those houses which use solid fuel must use a smokeless variety. Grass, flowers and trees provide a clean and healthy environment. In the past, new housing estates have carved their way through the countryside and have seemed to have little respect for it. In the New Towns care has been taken to keep the surrounding countryside unspoiled.

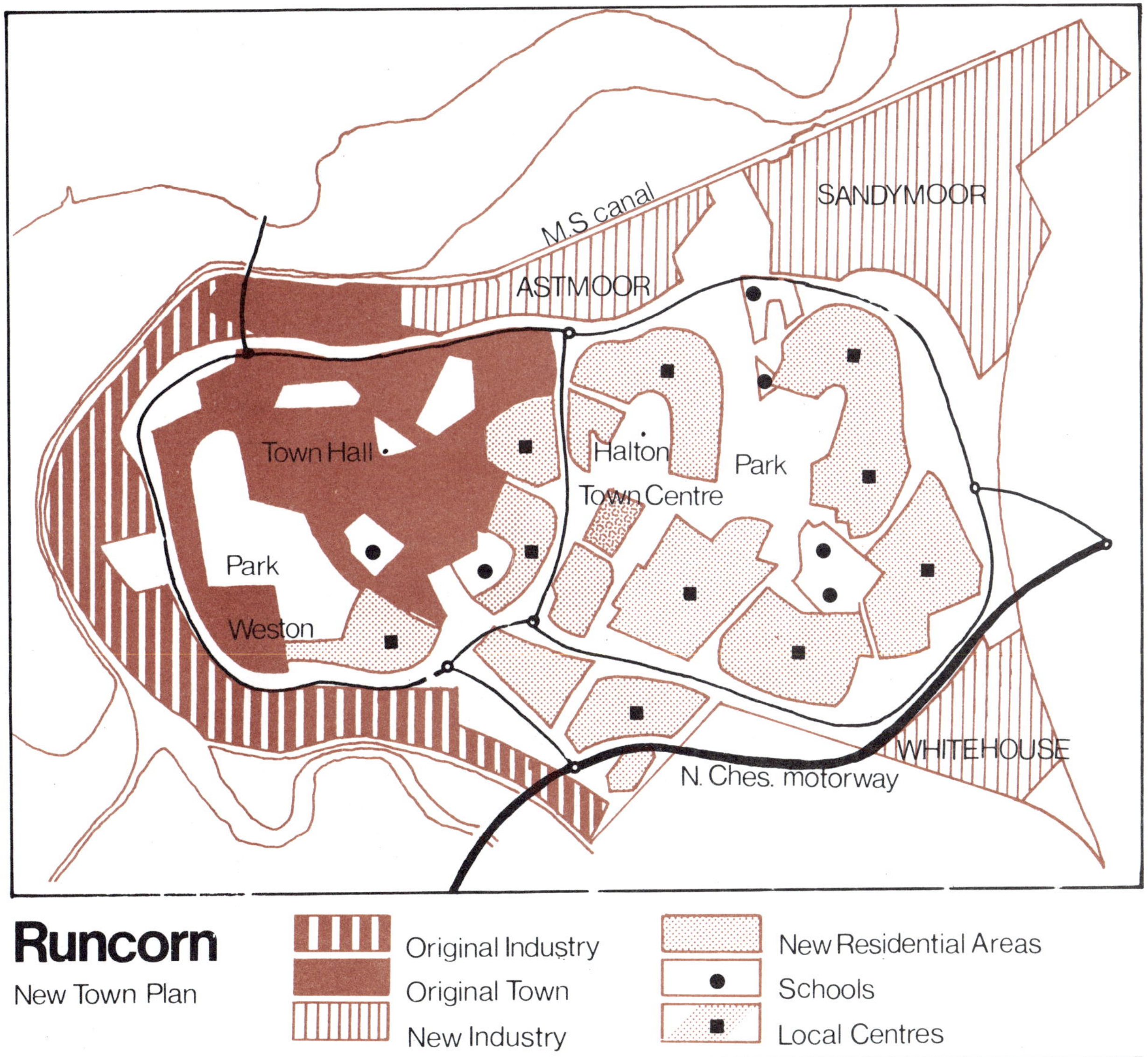

Runcorn
New Town Plan

Pleasant living conditions, Runcorn.

At **Runcorn New Town** the ancient Norton Priory has been preserved. The new residents are able to see how monks lived in days gone by. Norton Priory is well worth a visit.

Each New Town has a Town Centre and a Shopping Precinct. There are pedestrian areas where no cars can enter. There, people can walk around the shops in complete safety.

The New Towns have been planned so that people can live in a community. There are no giant tower blocks of flats where people can be isolated. Community centres, churches, youth clubs, and public houses are evenly spread.

New Towns have been built with the needs of the inhabitants in mind.

Above: 13th cent. coffin lid, Norton Priory.
Right: Pedestrian Shopping area, Shopping City.

Whereas the Government in London is responsible for the running of the whole country, local affairs are run from your Town Hall. There your Town or City Council meets to make decisions that may affect you, your family, your house, your street, your school.
But what is a Town Council and how does it work?
The Town Council is a group of men and women called **Councillors** whose job it is to represent the ward which elected them. Each town is divided into sections called wards. Every three years an election takes place to elect a councillor in each of the wards. There may be three or four candidates standing for election but only one is elected councillor. Each candidate is usually a member of one of the political parties (Labour, Conservative, Liberal, etc.).
A ballot is held to choose which candidate will be elected. People who have a vote (who are over 18 and whose names are on the Register of Voters) choose which candidate they would like to represent them. They go to a polling station to vote.

Find out if your school is used as a polling station; many schools are.
To vote, each person collects a ballot paper which bears the names of all the candidates. The voter secretly puts a cross next to the name of the person he wants to be elected. The ballot paper is then put into a ballot box. In this way, each vote is made in secret.
When the polling station closes, all the ballot boxes from every polling station in the ward are taken to a collection point for counting. There the boxes are opened and the votes for each candidate carefully counted. When they have been counted, the candidate with the most votes is declared the winner. It is this person who will then represent his ward on the Town Council.
Hold an election in your class. Choose candidates, make speeches about what you would do if you were elected. Make advertisements for the candidates. Find out what an electoral roll is—make one for your class. Make ballot papers and a ballot box and hold a secret ballot. Count the votes and declare a winner—the new "Class Councillor".

The Council

When all the Councillors have been elected for all the wards in your town or city they form the new Town or City Council. Some Councillors belong to the Labour party, some to the Conservative, some to the Liberal, some to other political parties, and a few are independents—that means they do not belong to any political party. One party will have the most Councillors. When the new Council meets it elects a leader to preside over all Council meetings. He is called the Lord Mayor (as in Liverpool), the Mayor (as in Bootle) or Chairman of the Council (as in Huyton-with-Roby). He or she is chosen each year to represent the Council legally. Nothing agreed at Council meetings can be put into operation without the Mayor's or Chairman's signature.

Find if your Council is led by a Lord Mayor, a Mayor or a Chairman. Try to find out more about his job and how he was elected.

The job of the Town Council is to make sure that we all have a wide range of services—like housing, education, public health facilities, refuse collection, sewage disposal, markets, parks, libraries, roads, lights, etc. To do this efficiently Committees are set up which are responsible for certain items. For example, there is a *finance* committee, a *housing* committee, an *education* committee, a committee responsible for *roads* and *lighting*, and another that looks after our *parks*. Clearly, there are many committees! Each Councillor sits on some of them and does his best to see that it provides the best amenities. Try to talk to your local Councillor. Find out more about how he was elected and how the Council is organised. Find out too which committees he sits on.

Finance.

Housing.

Education.

Money!

To provide all these services the Council needs a great deal of money—but where does it get it from? Some of the money comes from the entrance fees you pay when you go to the swimming baths and from fines on library books. A lot of money comes from rates. Every householder pays rates to the local Council.
Here is an example of a house which has just been bought. The new owner has been told that the rateable value is £100—that is the amount of money the Council would expect if they owned the house and rented it for a year. But the owner does not pay all of this £100 each year. The Council decides what the rate is—for this house it is 80p in the pound. So for each £1 of the rateable value the owner pays 80p. So altogether he pays:—

80p × 100 = £80 each year.

But most of the money needed to provide these services comes from grants from the Government in London.
All this money is organised by the Council's Finance Committee and the Treasurer. He is one of the many paid officials who carry out the resolutions passed in Council. Other such officials include the Town Clerk, the Engineer, Surveyor, the Director of Education and his Officers, Parks and Gardens Director, Medical Officer of Health, Housing Officer, Planning Officer, etc. They also advise Councillors of true facts—e.g. if a Councillor decided that your school needed a new gymnasium he would ask the Education Officer for details about your school's facilities. From this information he could argue a case in Council and you may get your gymnasium.

Roads and lighting.

Parks.

There are other paid officials, too, in each of the departments—teachers, baths attendants, park keepers, librarians, caretakers and cleaners, etc. But the biggest single item that money is spent on is education. Money is needed to pay for teachers' salaries, exercise and text books, repairing school buildings and paying for heat and light.

Find out how much money is spent by your school on text books alone. This will give you some idea of the money spent especially when you look in the telephone directory and find out how many schools for which your Council is responsible.

The Metropolitan District

Local Government is changing. There was a time when every town on Merseyside had its own Council, but now these Councils are combining to form larger units. The effect will be to draw Merseyside even closer together into a unit. Already the Police forces of Liverpool and Bootle have combined and you have read about the Merseyside Passenger Transport Executive which has combined the bus and ferry services once run by the separate Councils of Liverpool, Birkenhead and Wallasey. These are just two examples of how public services have come under the control of a wider authority than the old City, Town or Rural Councils. Why do you think this has been done? Find out the name of the Government Report that led to expanding the area controlled by Local Government bodies. Make a list of all the services you and your family make use of which are provided out of the rates. Supposing one of these amenities or services was withdrawn by, say, refuse collectors going on strike, how would this affect your life? Write a poem or a description of the kind of day it would be without such a service.

There are many people responsible for the smooth running of your school—not just the teachers, but the cleaners, caretakers, dinner ladies, welfare assistants, etc. Most of these people you meet every day.
Everyone working in your school is employed by your Town or City Council's **Education Committee.** This body also decides what kind of system your area follows. On Merseyside there is a variety of systems. If you lived in Wallasey you would go to a Primary School from five to nine. Then you would go to a Middle School from nine to thirteen. Then you would move to what is called a third tier school, which is like a Grammar School, from thirteen until you left school to go to work, or College, or University perhaps. In Kirkby, however, the system is different. If you lived there, you would go to the Primary School at five and stay there until you were eleven. Then you would transfer to a Comprehensive School until it was time for you to leave. What does Comprehensive mean? How does it differ from a Grammar or Technical School?

Find out what system your Education Committee operates. Try to draw a diagram to explain it.
All the paper, pens, pencils, desks, chairs and apparatus that you use in school have been paid for by the Education Committee. Millions of pounds are spent every year by your Education Committee. Liverpool alone spends £35 000 000 every year. Fifty-eight per cent of this goes towards paying the salaries of teachers and everyone else employed by the Education Committee. Forty-two per cent is spent on school building and repairs. You can work out how much money each of these percentages represents. Which ever way you look at it, it is a great deal of money.

Children working on a mural to brighten up their school.

Down town schools

In older parts of Merseyside many old schools are still in use. They are dark, dreary buildings. Some are more than a century old. At some of these schools the children have painted murals on the playground walls with the help of their teachers to brighten up the drab surroundings. These schools look out of place amongst the new flats and houses of the redeveloped areas but their history and traditions give them character. There may be some schools in your area whose names give a clue to their history. For example, there is Matthew Arnold Primary School in the Dingle in Liverpool, or Cowley School in St. Helens.

Many opportunities are offered by Merseyside schools. At **Colomendy,** near Mold in North Wales, there is an Environmental Studies Centre. Children can go there for long periods with their school to examine country life in detail. Many young people who are interested in music can join the many youth orchestras and choirs that exist on Merseyside.

Many schools are involved with linking themselves with the neighbourhood of which they are a vital part. Some have become community schools—they are used not only by their pupils but by the community in general. Their doors do not close at four o'clock but remain open all evening for parents and children, clubs and societies. In this way many more people are able to benefit from the use of this expensive equipment bought with public money. In the new estate of Netherley the Comprehensive School has become a lively centre for many different activities in the local community.

Above: Colomendy School.
Right: Netherly Comprehensive School. Playgroup.

What do you want to be?

When you leave school there are many paths that you can choose. Before you decide which path you should take, the Careers Officer from the Education Committee's advisory service visits your school to suggest possible careers. Merseyside's colleges have many opportunities to offer. There are several technical colleges which specialise in a variety of subjects, from plumbing to catering. One college even trains young people to be chefs on board ships. To study at a technical college you can either go full-time, or, if you are at work, you can go on a sandwich course, or on day release. A sandwich course involves studying full-time at the college for some weeks, then going back to work, then returning to the college. Day release involves studying one day each week at the college. For the rest of the week you would be at work. The North-East and Old Swan Technical Colleges specialise in these courses. But Birkenhead, Bootle, Kirkby and St. Helens also provide some. Find out what courses are offered by your local Technical College.
When you stay on at school and take O and A level G.C.E., there are plenty of opportunities for you to study on Merseyside.

Opportunity, opportunity!!

For those who wish to become teachers, Merseyside has many famous Colleges of Education. In Liverpool there are seven colleges. C. F. Mott, St. Katherine's, Christ's, I. M. Marsh, Ethel Wormald, Notre Dame and F. L. Calder (which specialises in Domestic Science). There are others outside Liverpool at Chester, Edge Hill (Ormskirk), Padgate (Warrington), and Cartrefle at Wrexham.
Liverpool has a Polytechnic too. A Polytechnic is really lots of different colleges which are organised together. These include the College of Commerce, the College of Technology, the College of Building and the College of Art. Together now, they make the Liverpool Polytechnic. Here you can study arts and technical subjects which lead to degrees. You can study such things as building engineering, commerce, business studies, surveying, computer technology, etc. The Regional College of Art is now part of the Polytechnic too. Many great artists, like Augustus John, have been associated with the art of Merseyside.
On Merseyside too is the enormous **University of Liverpool.** (The number of students attending in the year 1971–72 was 7 518.) The original Victoria Building was opened in 1892 but many of the buildings are new. They house the various departments where the students are taught, and where research is carried out. Several famous important discoveries have been made at Liverpool University. Some of them have improved the health of people throughout the world.

Professor C. A. Clarke discovered a way of preventing rhesus haemolytic disease. (A "fault" in the mother.s blood which caused babies to die if no treatment was available.)
Sir Ronald Ross worked at the School of Tropical Medicine from 1902 to 1918 on the treatment of malaria, a deadly disease suffered by people living in the tropics. It is largely due to the discoveries of Sir Ronald Ross that malaria is no longer a killer.
Merseyside Colleges and University offer a whole range of opportunities which suit all levels and all tastes. If you are about to leave school think about your interests carefully and then find out from your careers master and Careers Officer the best path to follow.

Liverpool University.

C5. Caring for people

Every community has to have people and places which care for its members who are in need. The most obvious people who are in need are those who find it difficult to look after themselves—the very young, the old, and the disabled. The local council provides many of these services with money paid for out of the rates.

Day nurseries are provided for very young children who are not old enough to go to Infants' School. These nurseries are staffed by specially trained nurses who look after the young children while their mothers are away. Some mothers go out to work either because they are the only breadwinners in the family, or to add to the father's earnings. They therefore have to take their children to the day nursery to be looked after while they are at work.

Children who may have been neglected by their parents are sometimes put in the care of the Local Authority. This means that your Council has to provide special homes run by nurses and teachers to look after them until the family problem is solved. Look in the telephone directory under your local corporation and find the section devoted to child care. You will be surprised how many homes like this are needed to look after these children who, for one reason or another, have not had the benefit of a secure family background.

There are also Clinics, paid for by the Council, where mothers can make sure their babies keep well and strong.

A day nursery.

Hospitals

The hospitals on Merseyside have a very high reputation. The **Royal Infirmary** in Liverpool, **Clatterbridge** on the Wirral, **Whiston** near Prescot are some of them. Some hospitals specialise in one field of medicine. This means that inside these hospitals highly specialised equipment can be concentrated, instead of being spread through a number of hospitals. Alder Hey Hospital in Liverpool specialises in children's diseases. There are hospitals which deal with particular illnesses, like the **Ear, Nose and Throat Hospital** also in Liverpool, and various chest clinics in the area. There are Maternity Hospitals, too, which give expert care to women having a baby.

Help the disabled!

On Merseyside there are between 15 000 and 20 000 people suffering from some kind of serious disability. They may be blind, or deaf and dumb. They may suffer from epilepsy or be diabetic. Or they may suffer from something more physically obvious—spina bifida, multiple sclerosis, muscular distrophy, or they may be spastic. There are many kinds of disability, and all those who suffer need particular care and attention. Many societies, clubs and welfare organisations exist to look after the disabled in Liverpool. **The Liverpool Association for the Disabled (L.A.D.)** is a partnership between the local authority and these various voluntary organisations. If a disabled person needs help, L.A.D. will investigate and contact the appropriate voluntary organisations. In this way the right kind of help can be obtained quickly. Some of the clubs run by caring citizens provide an opportunity for the handicapped to enjoy themselves. Many young people give up their time to help the handicapped to swim. Some handicapped people find floating in water restful and it gives them a sense of freedom for a short time.

You may have no difficulty in moving around your house, or a shop or a cinema, but to someone in a wheelchair, stairs make it impossible to move around such places. The corporation helps people like this to overcome these problems. Ramps built inside their own houses enable the wheelchairs to go up and down. Showers instead of baths enable the person in the wheelchair to wash. Also by means of a winch he or she can get in and out of bed from the wheelchair. Some shops and cinemas have made special provision for the disabled too. Walk around the shops and see how difficult it is for a person in the wheelchair. Find out what arrangements have been made for them.

The *mentally* handicapped also need help. Centres are provided by the Corporation and much is also done by voluntary bodies. You can find out more about this work if you contact some of the various Societies for mentally handicapped children that exist on Merseyside.

Senior citizens

Merseyside is constantly conscious of the need to look after the old who, in their time, have served the community so well. **The Old People's Welfare Council** does a lot for Merseyside's senior citizens. Rest Centres, daily clubs, outings, transport for those who are housebound have been organised. Advice on pensions and welfare is given. Those who are lonely, can have home visitors. Great care and attention is taken to see that the old are looked after properly.

Talk to old people and find out what welfare services they use.

There are also many old people's homes on Merseyside. Try to visit one and interview the Matron about the problems of looking after old people.

The hidden protectors

There are people employed by the Corporation who keep a constant watch over the kind of environment we live in. In their way they do a great deal to make sure our towns and cities are healthy places to live in. **Public Health Inspectors** inspect the food you eat and the shops where food is sold. They make sure that there is a high standard of cleanliness and hygiene.
Enquire into the alterations you would have to make to a building before you could open a café.
These public health inspectors form a "Doomwatch" team keeping a constant guard over the environment, protecting us from hidden dangers. For example, every ship entering the Mersey from a foreign port is inspected by the Medical Officer of Health to make sure it is not bringing diseases like typhus, cholera and smallpox to the port.
What dangers do you think threaten your environment? Find out as much as you can about pollution, about the way harmful waste products from industry and sewage is disposed of. Set up your own "Doomwatch".

Left: An emergency typhus demonstration.
Right: Health inspector boarding a ship.

Assignments for Theme C

Housing and Local Government

1. Things to discuss.

(i) What conditions made it possible for the rich people to live in expensive houses in Liverpool in the nineteenth century and why did they move out to the outskirts later on?
(ii) What consideration did the planners think of before deciding to build new towns on Merseyside?
(iii) What facilities provided by your local council do you make use of during the course of an average day?

2. Things to do.

(i) Make a model of a high rise block of flats near your home. Include in your model the nearby facilities available to the residents like open spaces and shops.
(ii) Visit a modern housing estate and draw up a plan of the layout of the area.
(iii) Design a house for either an old person or a disabled person. First visit an old people's home and interview the Matron to find out what you should consider when you are designing your house. If you decide to design a house for a disabled person you will receive help from the Liverpool Association for the Disabled or the Social Services Committee of your local council.

3. Things to find out.

(i) Many old houses are now used for different purposes from those for which they were originally intended. Look around your area and note any buildings that have changed hands over the years.
(ii) Which political party controls your local council at the moment? How does this affect the running of your town? Find out what the parties stand for. It might be an idea to invite a member of each party into your school to explain to you what they believe in and how this affects their decisions when they are in power.
(iii) Find out what steps are being taken in your area to prevent pollution and make the environment better for people. Cut out pollution stories from your local newspaper to help you collect the facts.

Theme D Work

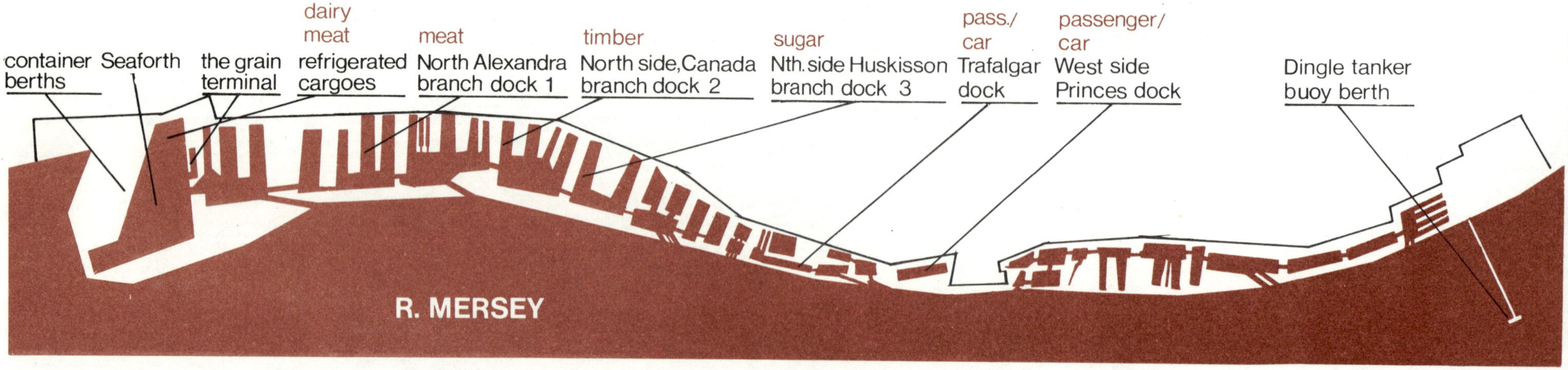

Top: The 'Empress of Canada' when she used to ply from Liverpool.

Below: Diagram of Liverpool Docks.

D1. The port and docks

Before the first dock was constructed in the eighteenth century, ships were unloaded in the pool or on to barges in the river. These barges were called "lighters" because they lightened the ships which were too big to get into dock and the men who worked on them were "lightermen". They were the fore-runners of today's dockers.

As trade grew the docks spread along both banks of the Mersey. **Herman Melville,** the American author who wrote "Moby Dick", described the docks in 1849. The picture he gives is recognisable even today.

"I beheld long China walls of masonry; vast piers of stone; and a succession of granite-rimmed docks completely enclosed. The extent and solidity of these structures seemed equal to what I had read of the old pyramids of Egypt. For miles you may walk along the riverside, passing dock after dock, like a chain of immense fortresses".

The docks were certainly fortresses. Outside, in the town, were areas of extreme poverty. Through these gates poured the dockers. The dockers were always casual workers. They had to report to the docks twice each day to see if there was any work. For this reason they generally lived within walking distance of the docks.

The work of the docker seems quite simple to the layman but it has great skills. It is generally done in gangs. Each gang is made up of its own experts. The first division is between the *holdsmen,* who work on the ship, and the *quay porters* who move cargo on the dockside.

The men on the ship have the following jobs:

1. The *holdsmen* down in the hold stowing or unloading cargo.
2. The *winchmen* operating the winches and derricks.
3. The *man at the rail* passing the word to the quay and co-ordinating the work of the two gangs.

The men who work on the ships are known as *stevedores,* while those who work on the quay are called *porters.* The quay men have the following jobs:

1. The *quay porters* who manhandle the cargo on the dockside.
2. The *weighers* who weigh each item of cargo.
3. The *checkers* who check off items as they come ashore.
4. The *markers* who write down details of each cargo in a register.

A docker's life used to be much tougher than it is even today. Until recently, most cargoes were placed in position by sheer physical strength. As the men grew older they were unable to do such heavy work. The gang system enabled them to be given lighter tasks such as the "man on the rail" or they were put on to making cargo nets to help in the lifting of cargo from the dockside.

When a ship is being loaded great care must be taken to see that the cargo is evenly balanced. This is the holdsman's job. He also has to take into account where each item of cargo will be unloaded. It would waste a great amount of time if the same goods had to be unloaded and loaded again in some foreign port because they had been placed in the wrong position when leaving Liverpool. To help the holdsman pack the cargo in the right order, he is given a "manifest". This is a list of all the cargo and the port to which it is destined.

Dockers working in a cargo-hold.

Since 1969 the docker has been employed by one firm. He gets a guaranteed wage even if there are no ships to unload. His hours of work are from 8 a.m. to 5 p.m. He has a break of a quarter of an hour between 9.30 and 10.30 a.m. This is called the "welt". The gang goes on working but the members go in ones and twos for their break.

Nowadays there is less manhandling of cargoes as machines are used. Proper canteens are provided. If protective clothing is required, the *employer* provides it.

Fork lift trucks, which are used in the holds and on the quays, have helped to take some of the sheer physical effort out of the job.

There is a growing move towards "container ships". Large containers which can be packed far away are taken by special lorries to the docks. All these containers are a standard size and they are easily loaded into specially constructed ships.

Changes on the docks

The container port depot is at Netherton, a mile or more away from the docks. Here containers are filled and unloaded. They are taken to and from the docks by lorries. At the quays there are huge cranes which span the berths and strange trucks which look like space-fiction insects. The containers are taken by the trucks to the quayside and there they are lifted into the hold by the cranes. This is the way of the future and the new dock at Seaforth has been built to handle cargoes in this manner.

Mechanical handling of cargo.

Ship taking on containers.

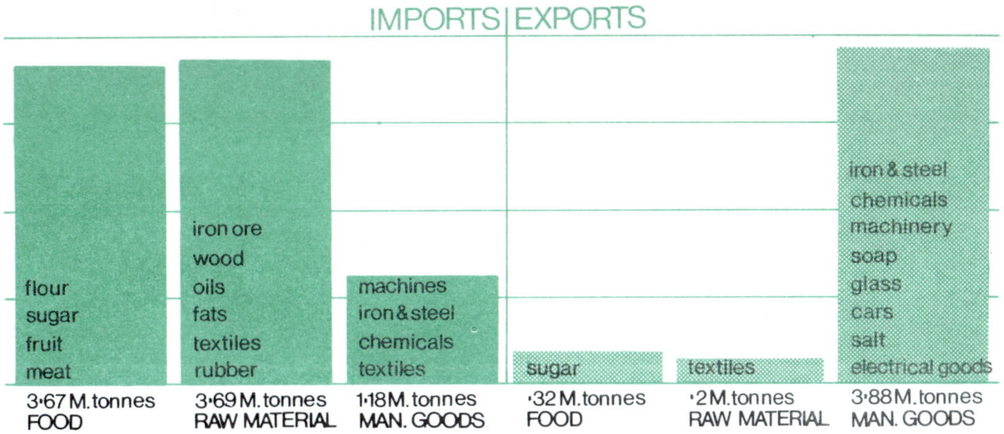

Where the trade comes from.

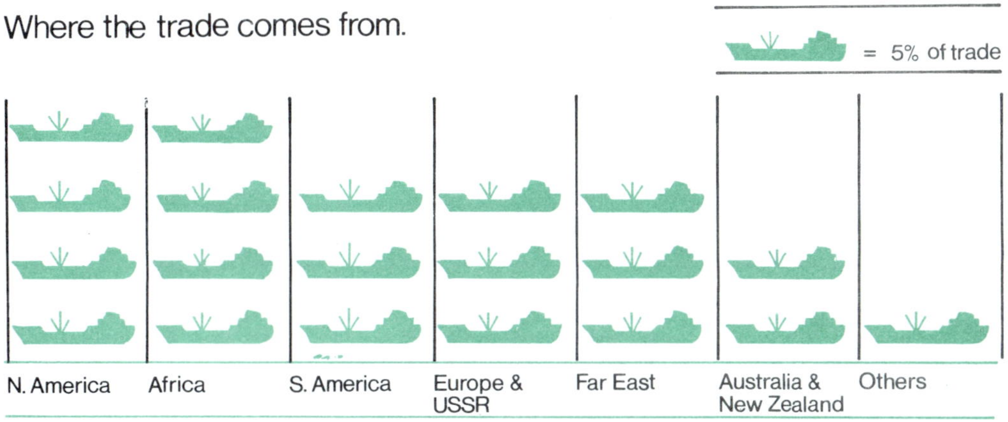

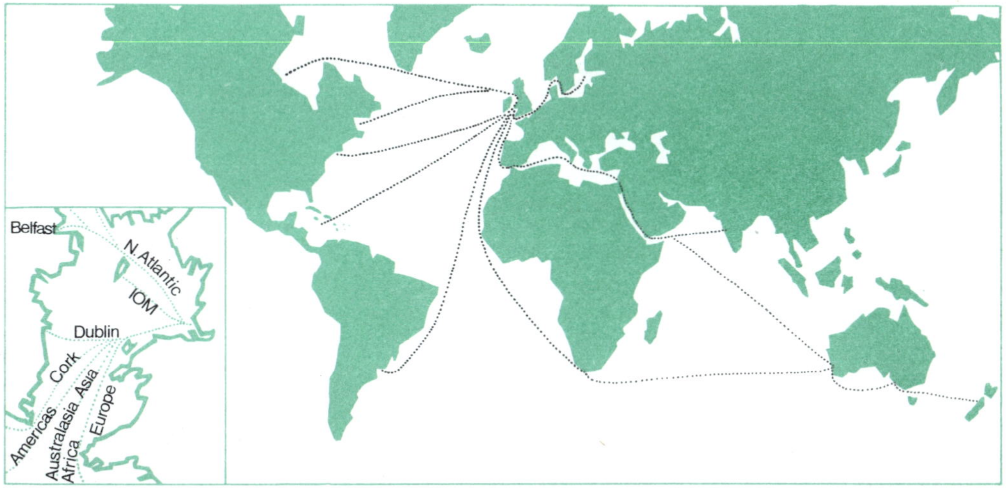

Trade

Liverpool is mainly an importing port. This means that we have more goods coming in than we send out. The dockers, in their work, move large amounts of goods each year. In 1967 8·6 million tonnes were imported and 4·4 million tonnes exported. As well as this 10 million tonnes of petroleum were unloaded at the Tranmere Oil Terminal. Different docks handle different goods. The Huskisson Dock has special facilities for handling SUGAR, the Alexandra Dock MEAT, the Hornby Dock BANANAS, Kings Dock FRUIT, Canada Dock TIMBER and Bidston Dock IRON ORE. In general the southern docks were concerned with trade with the West Indies and Africa, before they were closed in August 1972—now the ships use docks further north. The Central Docks are concerned with European and Irish trades, the North Docks with Australia, New Zealand and America, and the Birkenhead Docks with the Far East.

The ships that enter the port come from and sail to all parts of the world. If you look at this map of the world you can trace the dotted lines of the sea routes across the oceans and up the Irish Sea into the Mersey. The pattern of trade has stayed very much the same over the years. America and Africa still provide most of it as they have done in the past.

Shipbuilding and repairing

There has always been shipbuilding on the Mersey. As the docks spread along the Bootle and Liverpool side of the River, space on the opposite Birkenhead bank was used for shipbuilding. **William Laird,** a Scot, came to Liverpool in 1810 to get orders for his father's rope works. He stayed to found his famous shipyard at Birkenhead. Not only did he build the shipyard, he built houses for his workers. He laid out a pattern of well-ordered streets, unlike much of Liverpool, which grew up in a haphazard way. It is an early example of thoughtful town planning. The ships were at first of wooden construction but Laird soon changed to iron-made hulls. Many ships were built for the Navy. In a pantomime of 1861 at the Royal Amphitheatre, Liverpool, one character says:

"There was a time when England's proudest boast
Was of the wooden walls around her coast.
Now they're shot-proof iron built instead.
There's one upon the stocks at Birkenhead.
She, with her rifled Armstrong guns, I know,
Will give a good account to any foe".

This tradition has been carried on until today and such famous ships as the 'Ark Royal', the 'Devonshire' and some nuclear submarines have been made at Cammel Laird's, Birkenhead. One tragedy cast a shadow over the history of the yard. On 2nd June 1939 the submarine 'Thetis' sank while on trials in Liverpool Bay. There was a group from the Royal Navy on board with shipyard workers. One of the valves in the forward torpedo tubes let in water. Ninety-three men lost their lives in the disaster. There is a stone to the memory of all those who died at Holyhead, near to where the Thetis was grounded. There is also a communal grave in the town's Maeshyfryd cemetry. The Liverpool and Glasgow Salvage Company Limited who brought up the 'Thetis' still have the ill-fated submarine's bell.

Left: Cammell Laird's Shipyard.
Right: Launching the 'Orbita' at Cammell Lairds.

The sailors

Ships and sailors go together and Merseyside has always provided them in large numbers. At one time they were experts at handling sails but they soon became adapted to the new steam ships. When this changeover was taking place "schools" grew up to train men in the new skills. At one boarding house for sailors in Great Howard Street it was reported that men practised shovelling coal through a swinging barrel while being doused with water flung at them from buckets. This was to train them in the new trade (and very hot work) of stoker. Today real schools such as Riversdale College and the Nautical Catering College train present-day Merseysiders in the skills of the seafarer.
The sailors themselves rely on the skill of the Pilots who guide the big ships down the channels that lead into the Mersey. You can find out more about their work by reading "The History of the Liverpool Pilotage Service" by John S. Rees (published by the Southport Guardian). From it you will learn about the problems of negotiating the different channels.

Liverpool Pilot boat.

Wherever goods are exchanged there are men who are experts at buying and selling. Liverpool is a port where goods came to be sold. Round this activity has grown up the commercial centre of the city.
Standing at the Town Hall, you can look down Water Street past the massive banks to the imposing Pier Head. A glance down Dale Street reveals large insurance offices, like the **Prudential** and the **Royal,** and Building Society offices, such as the **Bradford Permanent, Woolwich Equitable,** the **Leek and the Westbourne.** Behind the Town Hall are the Exchange Flags where merchants bought and sold cargoes. In Old Hall Street was the Cotton Exchange which was once the centre of the world's cotton industry, while off Castle Street was the Corn Exchange. These massive buildings, homes of banks, insurance companies, shipping lines and exchanges show today the immense wealth that flowed into Merseyside as a result of shipping.

Shipping

Ships were always a source of wealth. The television series "The Onedin Line" shows this fact very clearly. Men would buy shares in a ship and if it had a prosperous voyage they would share out the profits. As the nineteenth century proceeded some men began to own more than one ship and in this way the great shipping lines were founded. **Samuel Cunard,** an American, won a contract to carry mails across the Atlantic and this was the start of his famous line. Later it joined with another famous line, the White Star Company. One of the ships of the White Star Line was the ill-fated **Titanic.** It is a very interesting though tragic story and you might like to find out more about this fine ship's last moments. You could start at the monument that tells some of the tale at the Pier Head. There is also a film called "A Night to Remember" which you should see if you can. In the Liverpool Museum you can find the only surviving ticket for this tragic voyage. It was bought by the Rev. J. Stuart Holden. His wife was taken ill at the last minute and so they did not sail on this doomed voyage.

Many other shipping lines have grown up on Merseyside. The **Brocklebank Line** has links with the Far East and the **Elder Dempster** Line with Africa. **Lamport and Holt** and the **Booth Line,** two lines which have now joined forces, sail to South America, while the **Ellerman Group** have links with Australia. You can find out some fascinating things about the shipping lines and the men who founded them. Such men as Holt, Bibby, Ellerman, Booth and Cunard made fortunes out of the ships that sailed from the Mersey. Nowadays with the growth of air transport fewer people wish to undertake the longer journey by sea. Most people seem to be in a hurry: for them, the sooner they arrive the better. The last liner to maintain a regular service across the Atlantic from Liverpool to Canada was The **Empress of Canada** which belonged to the Canadian Pacific Ships. This magnificent white liner has now been sold and Liverpool's last passenger link with the American continent has gone. The Empress of Canada now cruises in the Caribbean under the name of **Mardi Gras.** The Princes Landing Stage looks forlorn without its attendant luxury liners. Those liners still in use now ply from Southampton. Ships are still needed for cargo and the shipping lines keep the Mersey busy.

S.S. Titanic.

The 'Empress of Canada' in dock.

Insurance

Shipping has always been a risky trade and merchants and ship owners have used insurance to cover their losses.

Insurance works quite simply. If an owner had a ship worth £1000 setting out on a voyage, he found an insurer, and paid him £100 in case anything happened to the ship. If nothing happened, the insurer kept the £100 but if the ship was lost the insurer gave the owner £1 000. Your father does the same thing today with his valuable possessions such as his house or his car. If ships had not been as safe as they normally were, the insurer would obviously have soon gone bankrupt.

The men who took this "money" were called insurers or underwriters because they underwrote or agreed to compensate you for your losses. It is not surprising that many insurance companies grew up from these beginnings on Merseyside. They not only insured ships but buildings and property. The Royal Insurance Company which was founded in Liverpool paid out seven million dollars to the unfortunate house owners who had suffered in the huge San Francisco earthquake of 1906. Although they had no need to pay out, for it was classed as a natural occurrence and outside the terms of their policies, they still kept to their side of the bargain. This kind of straight dealing gave the Liverpool underwriters a very good name and they were respected throughout the world.

Friendly Societies

Another form of insurance, combined with saving, is the Friendly Society. Two very famous ones grew up in Liverpool. Poor people would pay a penny a week, and when they died, the Friendly Society would provide sufficient money for a decent burial. The **Liverpool Victoria** began in this way in 1843 and was soon followed by the **Royal Liver Friendly Society.** This Royal Liver Friendly Society built the Liver Buildings as its Head Office. It was on the advice of the Royal Liver that the first National Health Insurance Scheme was worked out by the Government. These two companies are the largest in the country though Liverpool Victoria has now moved to London.

The banks

Banks are not just places where we keep our money. They would soon go out of business if they locked our money away and gave it back when we wanted it. They make money work. They lend money to people who may have ideas for making more money themselves. They expect the money to be returned with a little more added to compensate for the service of borrowing. This amount, which is over and above the amount that was borrowed, is called interest. The banks of Liverpool lent money to merchants who wished to buy or hire ships or even purchase goods for trading. As trade prospered so did the banks. One of the famous banks of Liverpool was **Martin's** Bank. It was formed from Heywood's Bank, once the Bank of the Corporation of Liverpool, and the Bank of Liverpool. **Barclay's** now have taken over Martin's Bank. If you look carefully at some of the Barclay's branches on Merseyside you will see the crest of the Liver Bird. This means that that particular branch once belonged to Martin's Bank and still carries the crest that made Liverpool's Martin's Bank famous. You can see a plaque outside the Fenwick Street branch of Barclay's Bank in Liverpool, which explains the history of Martin's Bank.

Left: Panel recording the building of the first Head Office of the Liverpool Union Bank (Fenwick St.)
Right: The Liver Building.

As Liverpool's trade grew from the eighteenth century onwards ships brought raw materials from distant lands to the port. These materials like sugar cane, cotton and tobacco leaves were of no value in their raw form. They had to be manufactured into goods which could be sold for profit in the shops for the public to buy. Liverpool became both a great import centre and a great manufacturing city for processing these raw materials.

The men behind these businesses wanted their factories as near to the docks as possible to be near where the ships were unloaded. This would save money on transport and would mean, therefore, more profits for the business men. In this way, a band of industries and warehouses rose up next to the docks.

Tobacco

Merseyside's connection with America was established in the eighteenth century during the time of the "Slave Triangle" which you have already heard about. Among the raw materials brought back to Liverpool were cargoes of **tobacco** from the rich plantations of Virginia and Maryland.

Many Merseyside businessmen invested in these plantations, some even owned their own.

Tobacco was brought by importers who owned their own shops and who made their own blends of snuff, pipe tobacco and even cigars. Smoking tobacco soon became so popular that *nine* **clay-pipe makers** set up premises in the 1850's.

This advertisement appeared in a Liverpool paper in 1832:

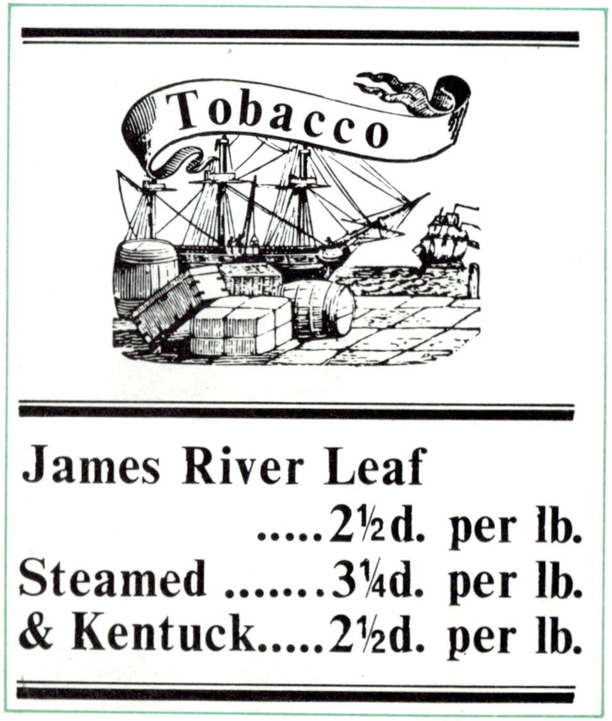

Left: An early tobacconist's shop.

The Government decided to put an import duty on tobacco. This did not please the importers who had to pay a tax on every pound (approx. ·453 kg) they imported to the Government. They began smuggling and using all kinds of ways to bring the tobacco into the country without paying duty, so much so that two inspectors were sent from London to check.

When the tobacco is landed today, it is put into **bonded warehouses** where it is stored. The word "bonded" means that the tobacco cannot be moved from the warehouse until duty has been paid to the Government. The bonded warehouse at Stanley Dock is larger than St. George's Hall and often more than £500 million's worth of tobacco is stored inside. Most of this value is the duty that has to be paid. The price of one tin of tobacco includes 72 per cent duty.

The tobacco remains in the bonded warehouse under Government seal for between eighteen months and three years. This means that when the leaves are imported they are very young so that they can mature in bond. Extra special precautions are taken to ensure accuracy. The weighing machines are checked sometimes as much as four times a day and work is constantly supervised. Even the sweepings on the floor are checked!

After the period of up to three years the tobacco can be "called forward from bond" by the manufacturers in Liverpool, Nottingham and Manchester. This means that Liverpool must have a good transport system and an efficient network of roads for quick distribution.

Some of the tobacco that is "brought forward from bond" may not be suitable. It cannot be used to make cigarettes or pipe tobacco and is considered as waste. This used to be burnt in an oven and the sweet smelling smoke used to go up a large chimney called the "King's Pipe". Today this waste is bought by firms who extract the nicotine to make **insecticides.** It takes, on average, 100 grammes of tobacco to yield 1 gramme of nicotine. Even the tobacco that remains behind after the nicotine has been extracted is used as a sort of **humus** by market gardeners. Nothing is wasted.

Two views of Ogden's tobacco factory.

Sugar

Large imports of raw sugar cane come to Merseyside from the West Indies. Britain has never been able to produce sufficient sugar beet to supply the home market with sugar, so over the years we have relied on **West Indian Sugar Cane.** Before the sugar can be manufactured into what we know as sugar it has to be refined. The first refinery in Liverpool was built in 1684. In 1872 Tate and Lyle set up their refinery near to the docks dominating all other small refineries that had grown over the years.

In 1970, 922 000 tonnes of sugar came to Merseyside. The sugar lands at Huskisson Dock where it is unloaded by four grab cranes onto conveyors which take the sugar to a massive silo where it is stored ready to be taken to the refinery. This silo holds 100 000 tonnes of sugar. The refinery has acted like a magnet to some industries, like the bakery industry, which needs a great deal of sugar. Many bakeries are to be found close to the refinery to cut down transport costs.

Milling

Seventy-five per cent of the nation's **wheat** comes from overseas. The other 25 per cent is grown here in Britain. In 1970 Liverpool handled 1 276 000 tonnes of grain. Much of it went to the many flour mills near to the docks.
Milling is no new-comer among industries on Merseyside. In several old views, like the one on page 83, you can see windmills standing in the fields surrounding Liverpool. They had to crush the grains between two revolving millstones and

Grab-cranes unloading sugar.

Sugar Silo at Tate and Lyles.

were driven by the strong west winds blowing off the sea.
There are still windmills at Bidston which are well worth a visit. Occasionally, too, you can see the remains of the walls of a windmill. Also, many names around Merseyside include the word "mill". There is Mill Street in Liverpool where once stood a line of windmills. This public house sign is at the top of Mill Lane in West Derby, once a rural village outside Liverpool. The public house is also on top of a hill which would be the ideal place for a windmill to catch the wind.
The local farmers and millers eventually could not supply the fast-expanding population of Merseyside, so wheat had to be imported.
Giant mills which grind the wheat to flour between enormous rollers have now replaced the primitive windmills and millstones. Most of the wheat today comes through **Brunswick Dock** from Canada.
It is milled nearby at such places as the famous **Scott's Mill.**

Left: An old view of a Merseyside Windmill.
Above: Modern flour-milling machinery.
Top: Public house sign at West Derby.

 Below: The grain loading system.
A giant grain suction gantry.

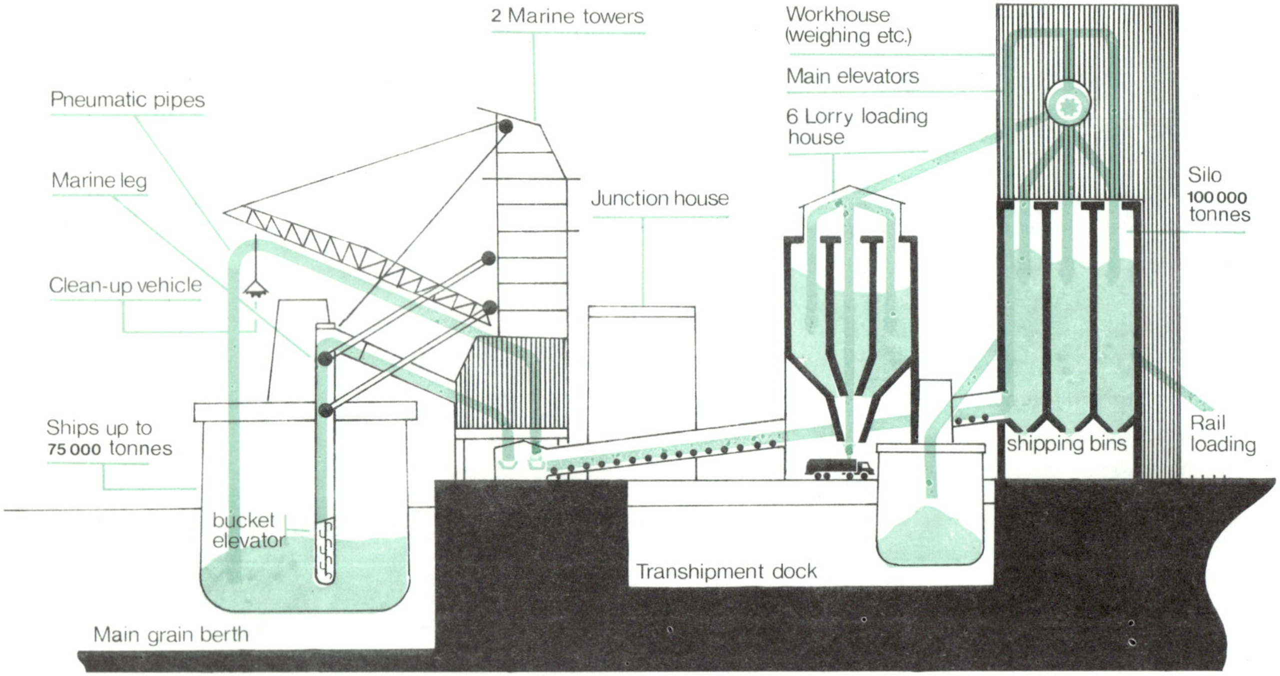

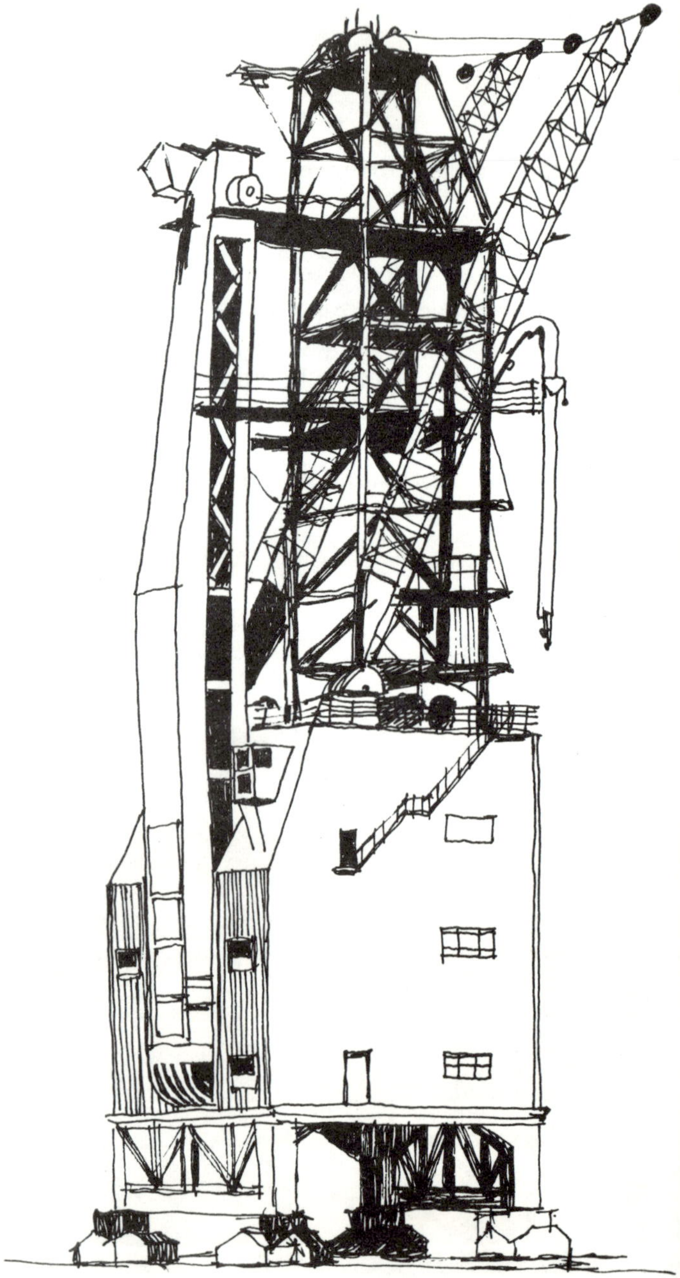

As Merseyside grew so did the imports of grain. Efficient methods were invented to enable the cargoes of grain to be unloaded quickly into the Mill. The new Grain Terminal in the new **Seaforth Docks System** will provide up-to-date facilities for unloading grain by using pneumatic pipes which suck the grain up from the hold of the ship like giant vacuum cleaners. Like sugar, grain is stored in large silos ready for the manufacturers to collect what they need to make into bread and cakes. Each silo can hold 100 000 tonnes of grain. Everything is automated and efficient.
Near to the Seaforth Grain Terminal there are sites for mills connected directly to the silos by a conveyor line.

Some of the grain that arrives in Liverpool is redistributed, either by road, by canal barge or by rail to other parts of Britain.
Within 150 kilometres of Liverpool there are **19 million** people living! This includes four out of seven of Britain's large conurbations and more than 70 towns with more than 50 000 people living in each. Merseyside's docks have become a valuable import centre, particularly for grain. Twenty-five per cent of Britain's unmilled cereals, and eighteen per cent of milled cereals are handled here and with the new grain terminal at Seaforth these percentages are bound to increase.

Seaforth grain terminal.

D4. Coal, glass, chemicals and soap

St. Helens, Widnes and Runcorn are part of Merseyside, although they have a different character from that of Liverpool. The people speak with a broad accent which belongs to Lancashire rather than the nasal tones of the Liverpudlian. These towns are associated with three industries which have played a very important part in the development of Liverpool and Merseyside as a whole: coal, chemicals and glass.

Miners working at the coalface.

Coal

If you look at this map you will see that the **South-West Lancashire Coalfield** included Prescot, Whiston and St. Helens. Coal has been dug here since before the sixteenth century. It is not surprising that after a period of nearly five hundred years of constant mining that the coal by now has almost run out. Yet at one time Liverpool depended upon this coalfield for its prosperity. As the Port grew so did the demand for coal for domestic purposes and also for the developing industries like **sugar-** and

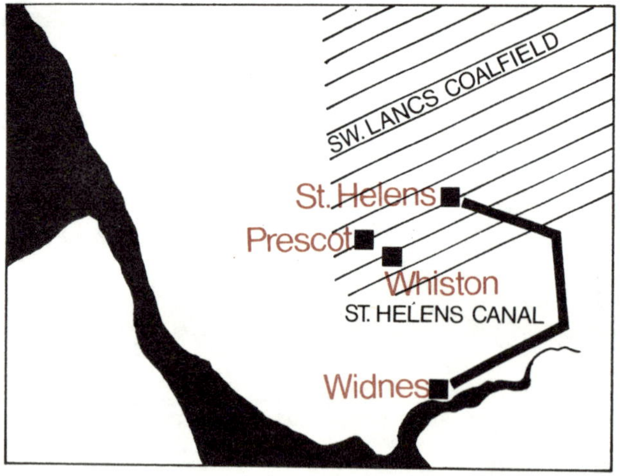

salt-refining. At first the coal was transported on horseback from Prescot to Liverpool, but this mode of transport was slow to meet the increasing demand for coal. Liverpool merchants therefore invested money in the construction of the St. Helens Canal. This canal was opened in 1757 and it was the first canal of Britain's Canal Era.

The canal stimulated coal mining in St. Helens. In the early days coal was mined to the North of the present town boundary at Windle and Laffak, near Carr Mill. As this coal became exhausted and the canal was built, mining moved almost to the centre of present day **St. Helens,** around the head or the end of the canal. One of these pits remained in production until 1968 and was the last pit to operate inside the boundary of St. Helens. This pit was the **Ravenhead Colliery.**

The coal fed the industries and hearths of Liverpool and gave rise to industries in St. Helens like the chemical, glass, iron and copper smelting and refining industries. The raw materials for these industries were brought to St. Helens from the Mersey by canal.

Look at the print of the Centre of St. Helens (top right) in 1879 and describe what it shows. Compare this print with the photograph below it of the same part of St. Helens taken recently. What has changed since 1879?

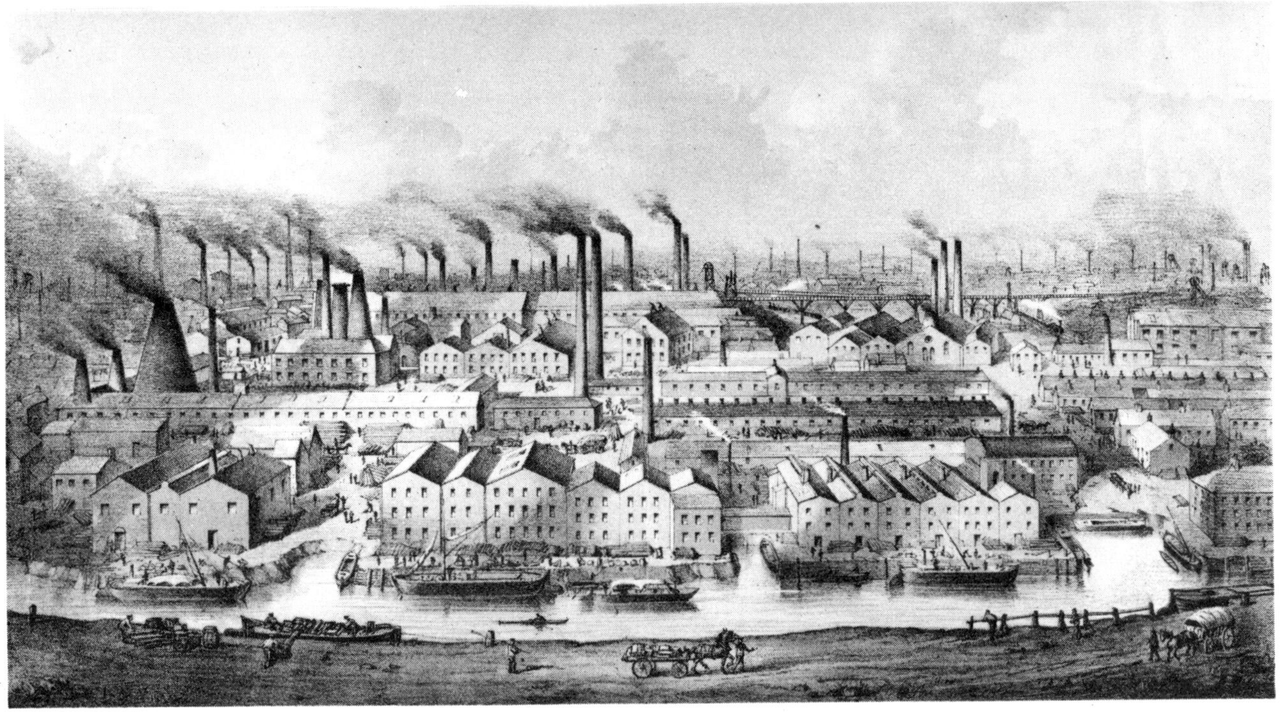

Conditions of work on the coalfield were much the same as on other British coalfields. The collier and his wife worked together and were paid by the amount of coal they dug out of the mine. In 1842 at Whiston Colliery, for example, the following were employed:—

965 men
50 women
396 boys and girls between the ages of thirteen and eighteen
192 boys and girls under the age of thirteen

The men hewed the coal with pick-axes and made the passages and roofs safe with timber cut to size with axes and saws. The women and children hauled the coal to the pit shaft and operated the ventilation door. Work underground was hard and dangerous. The miners used to say that "blood and bone was the price of coal". If you want to know what conditions were like down the mines, "Nine Centuries of Coal", a film made by the National Coal Board, will give you a clear idea.

Modern mining has had to follow the coal South of St. Helens and now the deep seams are being worked from three mines only: **Bold, Cronton** and **Sutton Manor.**

Above: St. Helens in 1879.
Left: St. Helens today.

Chemicals

The Chemical Industry started in St. Helens as a result of three men whose names are still associated with St. Helens and Warrington. Their names were **Muspratt, Gamble** and **Crosfield.** They brought the raw materials of salt and lime up the canal to the coalfield and manufactured a whole variety of chemicals in St. Helens. In 1891 these firms became the United Alkali Company and moved to Widnes. Later the firm became **I.C.I.** (Imperial Chemical Industries).
The modern chemical industry of the giant I.C.I. now extends from Widnes through Runcorn and Weston Point to Northwich and Winsford. The industry is based on Lancashire coal, limestone from Derbyshire and salt from the Cheshire salt fields. The salt was originally mined from the vast fossil salt lakes of the Triassic deserts that lie underneath Cheshire. Most salt is now found in the form of brine, and only the **Meadow Bank Rock Salt Mine** near Winsford still operates in the old way. Brine pumping has been important since 1924 around Northwich. The salt is obtained from bore holes.
The raw materials of this chemical industry are bulky, therefore cheap transport is essential. Three waterways have been important for carrying salt in the past—the St. Helens Canal, the Mersey and the canalised River Weaver. The Manchester Ship Canal and the Weaver are still important.
The most modern branch of the chemical industry is associated with petroleum:—

The I.C.I. at Weston Point.

Products of the chemical industry

Town	Chemical	Used in the manufacture of these commodities
Northwich	Alkalis	
	Soda Ash	Glass
	Caustic Soda	Soap, textiles, paper
Runcorn	Chlorine	Bleaches, plastics, antiseptics, fire-extinguishing chemicals, solvents
Widnes	Sulphuric Acid	Super-phosphate, fertilizers, rayon, dyes, explosives, detergents, films, paints

Glass

The glass industry was developed in St. Helens partly as a result of the physical advantage of the town's position and partly as a result of the enterprise of the Pilkington family.

The raw materials required for the manufacture of glass are:—

Coal
Silica (mainly from sand)
Soda Ash (from the chemical industry)
Limestone (from Derbyshire)

Coal for the glass industry was readily available in St. Helens and huge deposits of wind-blown Shirdley Hill sand occur to the North and West of the town. This sand is comparatively free from iron content and this means that glass produced in St. Helens is not discoloured. The greenish colour in some glass is due to the iron content. All these materials were easily gathered together in St. Helens and there were several glass factories in the area before the **Pilkington Brothers** set up their factory in 1826. They were so successful, however, that by 1842 their works were said to be the largest of their kind in England.

Here are some facts about the present day Pilkington Group. It is now a world-wide enterprise with forty subsidiary and associated companies in more than twelve countries.

The company makes:—

Float glass—windows for all types of buildings
Safety glass—"Triplex" glass for motor cars
Glass fibre—insulation and construction
Pressed glass—television screens, glass bricks
Optical glass—spectacles, cameras, electronics, optics

Pilkington's sells £100 million's worth of glass each year to 100 countries. The St. Helens' furnaces consume 7500 tonnes of local sand each week. Over one hundred other raw materials are needed, however, to make glass. To find out the whole story of glass-making, a visit to the **Glass Museum** at Pilkington's is essential.

D5. Soap at Port Sunlight

The massive soap and detergent factory of Lever Brothers can be seen very clearly from the main Birkenhead–Chester road in the Wirral. Between the factory and the road is **Port Sunlight,** the town that grew hand-in-hand with the factory.

Port Sunlight is really a dream made true. It was the dream of one man—W. H. Lever—who turned a desert of mud and slime into an oasis of a thriving factory and picturesque houses.

William Hesketh Lever had always had tremendous energy and great ideas. He was born in Bolton in 1851 and began his working life in his father's wholesale grocery business. His job was to travel around the area getting orders from shopkeepers. But he was so successful at this, his father could not cope with the flood of orders that his son obtained! Lever then moved to Wigan and opened his own wholesale grocery business—he was 22 at this time.

His connection with the soap industry really began in 1885 when he bought a soap works in Warrington. He used his energy and ideas to turn this into a very prosperous and productive venture. In June 1886 this works produced only 29 tonnes of soap each week; but by December 1887 weekly production had risen to 450 tonnes. At this time soap was made from tallow (melted fat). But Lever used vegetable oils instead. These oils made the soap creamier.

Lever also introduced new selling techniques. Instead of being cut off a block of raw soap in the shop, Lever's soap was made to look attractive. He called it **'Sunlight Self-Washer',** a name which caught the buyer's attention. So, too, did the attractive wrapping paper around the soap. In this way Sunlight became very popular soap.

W. H. Lever.

Expansion

Lever's energy soon spread the fame of Sunlight to Liverpool, Manchester, then to Plymouth, London and north to Scotland and on through the United Kingdom. He even exported it to Europe, South Africa and Australia.
The demand for Sunlight soap became so great that the Warrington factory could not cope. A new site for a larger factory was needed. Lever found such a site near to the muddy **Bromborough Pool.** Here, with his brother J. D. Lever, the new factory was to be built. But to many this site was ridiculous. It was described as being:
"mostly but a few feet above high water level and liable at any time to be flooded by high tides and thus to become undistinguishable from the muddy foreshore of the Mersey. Moreover, an arm of Bromborough Pool spread in various directions filling the ravines with ooze and slime. A few houses, or shanties, were scattered on the higher portions whose conditions as regards sanitation were not fit for human settlement".
But to a man of Lever's vision it offered a challenge. He said, as the foundations were being dug in 1888:
"It is my hope—some day to build houses in which our work people will be able to live and be comfortable in, semi-detached houses with gardens back and front in which they will be able to know more about the science of life than they can in a back slum, and in which they will learn that there is more in life than the mere going to and returning from work and looking forward to Saturday night to draw their wages."

Port Sunlight at the turn of the century.

Better conditions

This was a remarkably revolutionary idea—many families at this time were still living in slums and still drawing water from public pumps. But at Port Sunlight (the new village was called after the original Sunlight soap) the workers would have attractive houses, hot and cold water in their homes, well planned gardens and amenities.
And so the village and the factory grew together. Of the 25 hectares Lever first bought, 15 hectares were used as land for houses, and 10 for the factory and offices, and 500 tonnes of soap were produced each week. By 1925 Port Sunlight comprised of 90 hectares, of which 55 were taken up by the village and 35 by the factory and offices, and production had risen to 4000 tonnes of soap per week.

Port Sunlight village was extremely well planned from its beginning and great care was taken to ensure the welfare of the people. Houses were built in attractive groups of three to seven, and no two groups were alike. The density of houses per hectare is no more than 3, but at the turn of the century when Port Sunlight was growing, it was usual to find 20 houses per hectare in industrial areas. Each house has gardens and there are many open spaces. All these are tended by paid gardeners.
There are many clubs and leisure organisations to involve the community; social clubs, a library, a theatre and a licensed hotel, etc. In 1922 the Lady Lever Art Gallery was built—it is well worth a visit.

Left: Port Sunlight Village.
Above: The Lady Lever Art Gallery.

How soap is made

The vast factory turns out soap and domestic detergents which are well known in Britain and exported to countries where Lever factories are not part of the local industry. All the soap products are made from "neat soap". This is made from fat and caustic soda. One of the by-products of this is glycerine. The "neat soap" spreads through the factory in pipes. Every process is controlled automatically. The factory makes four basic products:

(*a*) soap,
(*b*) soap flakes,
(*c*) soap powder,
(*d*) soapless detergent powder.

The factory does everything involved in the production of these soaps and detergents. Lever Brothers Limited is now part of the Unilever Group of companies, whose interests include plantations, margarine and other edible fats, quick frozen foods and ice cream, dried and other packaged foods, flavourings, perfumes, chemicals and packaging. Several of these varied industries are represented by factories at Port Sunlight or nearby at Bromborough.

Lever Brothers and Port Sunlight are known throughout the world. Look at the wrappers and containers of the soaps and detergents in your home and find out which are made by Lever Brothers.

In the nineteenth century Merseyside had "boomed". Liverpool Docks handled a wide variety of imports and exports. The imports included sugar, wheat, tobacco, timber and oilseed. Processing industries grew up behind the docks to refine sugar, crush oil seeds and mill timber and flour. Merseysiders, too, were very dependent on imports because they provided them with work.

Some of these old-established industries declined in time and this meant that on Merseyside unemployment became a serious problem. To combat this, new blood had to be injected.

The new blood that was injected was that which the new idea of an **Industrial Estate** brought along. Many industrial estates were built around the boundaries of Liverpool in an attempt to solve the problem of unemployment by attracting firms to come to the area to make use of the facilities offered by the industrial estate. At Kirkby, where there was an Army Ordnance Factory making ammunition during the War, the Liverpool Corporation leased the original building to firms wishing to make a start on Merseyside.

This was to become a modern industrial estate—one of the largest in the country.

To attract industries Merseyside offered three things:—

(*a*) a large work force so that manning the factories would offer no problem;
(*b*) grants of money to any firm setting up premises on the estates. The money would go towards building the factory and equipping it with all the machinery that would be necessary;
(*c*) a good network of road and rail communications.

So, many firms brought new industry to Merseyside avoiding dependence on the old port industries. The bright new factories produce a great variety of commodities.

Many are concerned with consumer industries—they manufacture goods which you and your family buy. Furniture, paints, cameras, are some of the items made. At Kirkby there is a large creamery and this is of course where **Pendleton's** Ice Cream comes from. Other foods are processed nearby, including the tinning of cooked meats.

You will not find *heavy* industries like coal mines or steel works on these estates. All the factories are clean, modern and *light*. They stand in well-laid sites with lawns and gardens. Windows are plentiful and let in plenty of light by which the workers can see to operate the modern machinery.

These industrial estates have grown alongside housing estates which house the men and women who work there. Each is dependent upon the other.

Speke, Kirkby, Skelmersdale, Netherton, Ellesmere Port and **Warrington** are just a few industrial estates on Merseyside. Visit one near your home. Study the layout and what the factories manufacture.

Motor car industries

You have seen the figures for the increase in the number of cars on the roads of Britain during the last thirty years in Theme One. You have also seen in Theme Two how the motor car has affected the planning of motorways on Merseyside. Everybody wants a car and to help meet this demand the giant factories of **Ford, Vauxhall** and **Standard-Triumph** motors have come to Merseyside. They came because of the large labour force, good road and rail communications and suitable land available to build large factories. These are some of the reasons why these factories were built. There is one more important reason. The factories were encouraged by the Government to come to Merseyside. Find out why this came about.

Standard-Triumph Motors, a part of the British Motor Corporation, set up their two plants on the Speke Industrial Estate, Ford at Halewood, just on the border of the Speke Estate, and Vauxhall at Ellesmere Port, on the old Hooton aerodrome, the home during the last World War of a fighter squadron of the R.A.F.

When these motor companies moved to Merseyside they had to train the new workers, who had never worked in a motor factory before, to use the modern automatic machines and to work the assembly lines.

Each of these new factories covers hundreds of hectares. Inside there are separate departments, or 'shops' which are responsible for one part of the assembly of a motor car. Making a motor car is like putting a jigsaw together. As the car passes along the assembly line so all the pieces that have been made in the various shops are added on.

The shape of the car begins in the *Press Shop*. Here steel plates are cut into the correct lengths by automatic guillotines. The steel plate is then taken to the presses to force the steel into the various shaped panels that make up a car body, the two sides, the front ends, the rear and the roof.

Next door to the *Press Shop* is the *Body Shop* where the panels are welded together to make a shell. One single shell may need as many as 5 000 spot welds. Most of the welding is done by automatic welding machines. Doors, boots and bonnets are fitted here also, before the "body in white", as the steel shell is called, goes on to the next stage.

Far left: The Vauxhall factory.
Left: The Standard–Triumph factory.
Below: The press shop at Vauxhall's.
Right: Welding in the body shop.

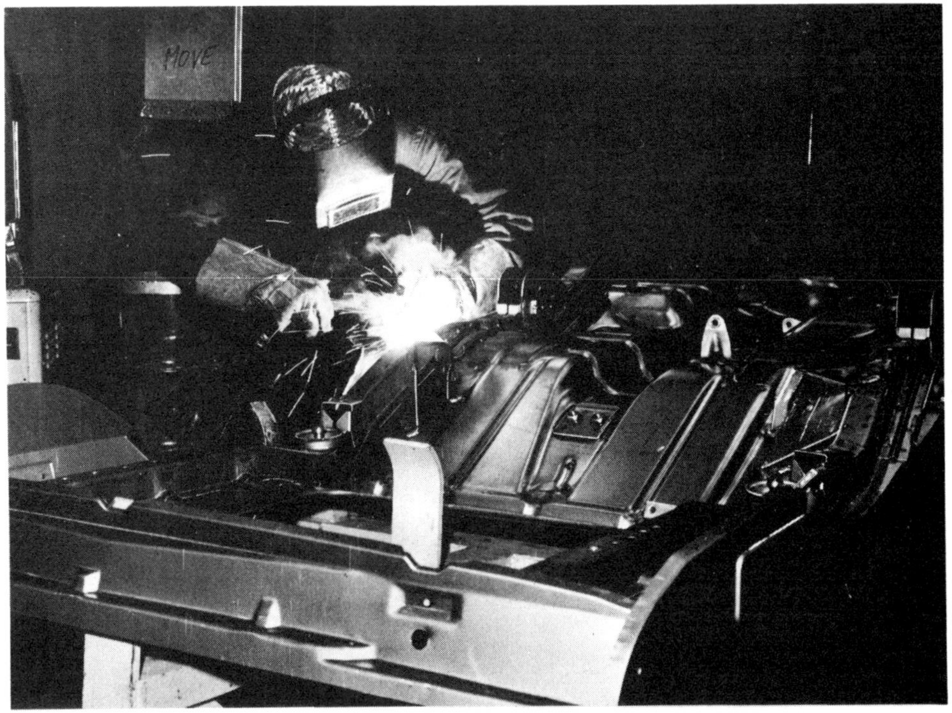

At the *Paint Shop* the cars are protected. The steel shells are made rust proof. After all the grease has been washed off, they are "primed". The cars are automatically dipped into enormous tanks of primer paint. They are dipped to ensure that every concealed corner of the car is protected. Then they are sprayed by automatic spraying machines which apply coat after coat of waterproofing protective paint. Those parts of the shell which are not reached by the spraying machines are sprayed by hand. Again this ensures that the whole body is protected.

The shells are dried in giant ovens. At last they are ready for their lustre coatings of hard wearing acrylic lacquer paint. Before they leave the *Paint Shop* the shells are undersealed and their undersides are sprayed with a bituminous compound which prevents corrosion from salt, spray and anything else thrown up from the road.

The next stage is the *Trim Shop*. Here the bare shells are now ready to collect their "trimmings". As they progress slowly along the "trim line", windows, seats, carpets, lamps, instrument panels are all put in their place. As many as 80 separate items have to be fitted here at separate "stations"—each station being responsible for a certain job.

Many of the items that the bodies collect on the Trim Line come from other factories scattered throughout the country. They are delivered to the factory daily by road and rail. It is vital that the car factory is not cut off from this supply, otherwise production will be held up and the assembly line will have to stop.

Several of the firms that make certain parts of a car's trimming have moved to Merseyside to be near these giant car factories.

Usually a separate building houses the *Machine Shop* which produces all the mechanical parts of the car—the engine, the gear-box, axles and transmission. Because so many are needed and such complicated operations are involved in their construction, they are made automatically by high precision machine tools.

When all the mechanical parts have been collected together they are carried by conveyor to the assembly building where they will join with the body shell.

As the completed bodyshell moves along the conveyor, the mechanical section is lifted into position. Wheels are fixed, petrol, oil and water put in, and the car is ready.

Before the car is allowed out of the factory, it is tested and adjusted to make sure it is in perfect condition. It is driven onto rollers and "motored" It is sprayed with water to check for leaks and finally it is given a wax polish. The car is now ready for delivery by road, rail or sea. Vauxhalls export their Viva cars to many countries through the docks at Ellesmere Port. The cars in this photograph are bound for Canada.

Extreme left: The paint shop.
Far left: The trim shop.
Left: Engine assembly in the machine shop.
Below: Vivas for export to Canada.

Fords at Halewood export 50 per cent of their total production of Escort and Capri cars through the Liverpool Docks.
To distribute the cars to other parts of the British Isles Fords use 35 trains a week. The cars are transported by "carties" or car flats.
Many millions of pounds have been invested by these firms. They have been encouraged to come to Merseyside where there was a large unemployment problem.

The Ford factory at Halewood.

Petro chemicals

Many of the ships that use the River Mersey are oil tankers, like the one in the photograph. They bring crude oil from South Africa and North Africa. Their long journey ends at the giant oil terminals on the Wirral. Their vast loads are discharged at Ellesmere Port, Stanlow and Tranmere.

As larger and larger tankers have been launched to carry more and more oil, ports have found it increasingly difficult to cope with them. Their vast size makes it difficult for them to berth and turn around.

At **Ellesmere Port** tankers could once sail a short way up the Manchester Ship Canal and berth alongside the refineries. In 1954, as the tankers were built larger, the Elizabeth II Dock was constructed at the entrance of the Manchester Ship Canal and crude oil was pumped through a pipeline to the refinery.

But today's tankers are so large that they have to berth at the end of long piers stretching out into the Mersey at **Tranmere.** Tankers of almost 100 000 tonnes can be berthed there and their enormous cargoes pumped into the refinery.

Most of the major oil companies have refineries at **Stanlow.** Esso, Burmah, Mobil and Shell are all to be found there.

At the refinery the oil is processed and made into many of the products vital to mankind—petrol, aviation fuel for aeroplanes, marine fuel for ships, each of different grades to suit the special need. Lubricating oils, waxes and a vast quantity of chemicals for other industries are also produced.

The largest ship to enter the Mersey, the Shell tanker 'Melo' at Tranmere.

Virtually none of the oil is wasted. The oil is moved around the refinery in a maze of long pipes which give it a space-age appearance. Towers stand like rockets on their launching pads.

The petrol that is refined is then distributed by road tankers which supply garages and petrol stations.

Oil refining and the petro-chemical industry are very necessary for today's way of life. They have helped in the growth of Ellesmere Port so much so that its setting has been represented in the Borough's coat of arms.

The wavy lines represent the River Mersey. On the shield, the vertical line represents the Manchester Ship Canal, and the black horizontal line represents an oil pipeline.

Oil refinery at Ellesmere Port.

Assignments for Theme D

Work

1. Things to discuss.

(i) (*a*) What advantages will container traffic bring to the import and export trade?
(*b*) For what *sort* of goods would you use a "container"?

(ii) How has Merseyside overcome the difficulties resulting from the run-down of the traditional industries like cotton importing and coal-mining?

(iii) Why did the chemical industry grow up around Runcorn and Widnes?

(iv) How had the petro-chemical industry adapted to the increasing use of giant tankers?

3. Things to find out.

(i) Find out from your local Education Committee what course and opportunities are available and where to young people leaving school.

(ii) Make a list of all the shipping lines which use Liverpool and Birkenhead Docks. What cargoes do they carry, and to and from which countries? The Education Officer of the Mersey Docks and Harbour Company will be able to help you.

(iii) Find out how many foreign countries have banks or consulates in Liverpool. You will be able to find the consulates from the telephone directory. Why do you think these countries are represented in Liverpool and not in others?

2. Things to do.

(i) Make a model of a ship being unloaded. Make a list of the different jobs done by the men working on the docks. Take care to pay attention to detail like the kind of cargo being discharged. Remember also that a visit to a dock will help you to collect the details you will need. (Before you visit a dock you must obtain a pass from the Mersey Docks and Harbour Company.)

(ii) Make a frieze of the River Mersey from Widnes to Seaforth showing the docks on both sides of the river. Use the map of the docks in Theme D1 to set you off. Remember there are docks at Runcorn, Garston, Ellesmere Port and the Manchester Ship Canal. When you have marked each dock fill in the cargoes each one handles.

(iii) Pay a visit to the Dock Road. Make a survey of where the lorries come from. Also note what they are carrying.

Liverpool v. Everton.

Every Saturday, from August to May, Merseysiders meet either at Anfield, home of **Liverpool Football Club,** or across Stanley Park at Goodison where **Everton** play. Two Saturdays a year all the football supporters on Merseyside meet at the derby (local) game when Liverpool and Everton play each other.

Football has been popular with Merseysiders for almost a hundred years. Everton was the original club. It started as a Sunday School football club called St. Domingo's. In 1891 some members of the Everton Club split away to form the club which was to become Liverpool F.C.

There is still great rivalry between the two big Merseyside sides. Red and blue take on a special loyalty for football supporters in Liverpool. The blue shirts of Everton have produced some great players, past and present. Tommy Lawton was one of the greatest centre forwards of all time. Dixie Dean also became a household name in his time. Every football supporter knows the present-day Everton team off by heart.

The red shirts of Liverpool also have legendary players of the past. There are Billy Liddell, who also played for Scotland, and Roger Hunt, who was one of the players in the 1966 England team who won the World Cup.

Every Saturday in the football season thousands of pounds change hands at the turnstiles. The big clubs like Everton and Liverpool can attract crowds of anything up to 50 000. Other teams in the football leagues also attract crowds, not quite as large as the big clubs perhaps. **Tranmere Rovers, Southport** and **Chester** also play in the Football League. You might be able to find old programmes involving Merseyside teams. They most probably will give you charts and attendance figures. You can make a graph to show the comparative popularity of these teams. Once you have drawn the graph, are there any other conclusions you can draw? For example, does the team's success or failure affect "the gate"?

Not everybody is content merely to watch football on Merseyside. In Liverpool alone, 268 amateur teams play for the fun of it on a Saturday and Sunday on as many as 92 Corporation pitches. If you look in the sports pages of your local paper you will discover there are many amateur leagues in existence on Merseyside.

Rugby League

In places like St. Helens, Wigan and Widnes, Rugby League is very popular. The supporters get just as passionate as the followers of football. Rugby League has never taken on in Liverpool or the Wirral. It remains a sport which belongs to Lancashire towns on Merseyside. Why is this so do you think?

The Grand National

One annual sporting event that has a big association with Liverpool is the **Grand National.** The racecourse is actually in **Aintree** and every March thousands of people come from all over the world to watch the horses and jockeys soar over the fences. Some of the fences have interesting names like **'Beecher's Brook'** or **'The Chair'.** Can you find out how these got their names and how high they are? Every year there is talk of selling the Aintree course for building. If that ever happens, and the Grand National is transferred to another racecourse, it will mean a break with history stretching as far back as 1836.

Other sports

Football, Rugby League and horse racing are the sports that attract crowds. There are less popular sports which some Merseysiders nevertheless enjoy. Cycling is one. In the summer at the stadium in Kirkby outside Liverpool, you can see cyclists riding round the track. There are thirty active cycling clubs on Merseyside some of them like **Kirkby Cycling Club, East Liverpool Wheelers** and **Liverpool Mercury Racing Club** are very well-known. Kirkby Cycling Club has many British Champions.

E2. A chance to meet

In the many **swimming baths** in the area many champions like **Sheila Ratcliffe** have learnt to swim, later to take on the rest of the world in the Empire, European and Olympic Games.
There are also the **boxers** past and present who have been born and bred on Merseyside. The Stadium in Liverpool used to be famous for its championship fights, but not so much now perhaps as in the past.
Some people prefer a more leisurely relaxation. Because Merseyside is on the coast it is not surprising that there are opportunities for people to **sail.** Hoylake, West Kirkby and Southport are popular yachting centres.

Weekends away

Merseyside schoolchildren in recent years have learned to enjoy other sports that have taken them outside the city to places like the Lake District and North Wales. Many local authorities and some schools even, have bought houses or old barns where young people can stay overnight while they spend their holidays enjoying the thrill of **climbing, walking** or **canoeing.**
Merseysiders enjoy their sport. Find out what sports you can enjoy in your area.

Merseyside is made up of a complicated mixture of people of different races, backgrounds and religions. Yet despite the differences they often come together.
One place where people meet is in the shops. In the older parts of Merseyside the shopping centres are on main roads. In other more modern parts shopping precincts have been planned. These are set well away from busy roads. The shoppers can walk from shop to shop without having to cross roads. What kind of shopping centre do you have near your home? Make a plan of the shops and point out what each one sells. Does your shopping centre offer everything that your family needs? If it does not, how does it affect your mother's shopping?

One of Merseyside's fine swimming baths.

Shopping

Perhaps the most important precinct on Merseyside is in Liverpool. It is called the St. John's Precinct. It serves the whole of Merseyside. Why do you think people from outside Liverpool come to the St. John's Precinct?

In some places on Merseyside the market is a popular place for bargain-hunters. Garston, Birkenhead, Frodsham, Chester, Ormskirk and Runcorn are all places where markets are held. Some of these markets date back to the Middle Ages when the farmers used to come to town to sell their goods. One very old market in Liverpool is Paddy's market.

Paddy's Market.

St. John's Precinct.

Liverpool Show

Another popular place for people to meet is the Liverpool Show. Ever since 1949 the Show has been held every July at the Mystery Park in Wavertree. The Park is called "The Mystery" because nobody seems to know who gave the land to the City of Liverpool. At the Liverpool Show you can see all kinds of exhibitions, flowershows and show jumping competitions. Usually there is one spectacular attraction which pulls in the crowds. A few years ago there was an American moon module on show. There are other big shows to go to in the summer.
The **Southport Flower Show** has been a national attraction since 1924. The Cheshire Show also draws the people of the Wirral to see the local farmers show off their prize animals. There are also smaller shows and festivals that bring communities together. Parts of Liverpool like Speke, Toxteth, Childwall and Anfield hold Neighbourhood Festivals where people show their paintings and processions are organised. Wallasey and Crosby also have their own Arts Festivals.

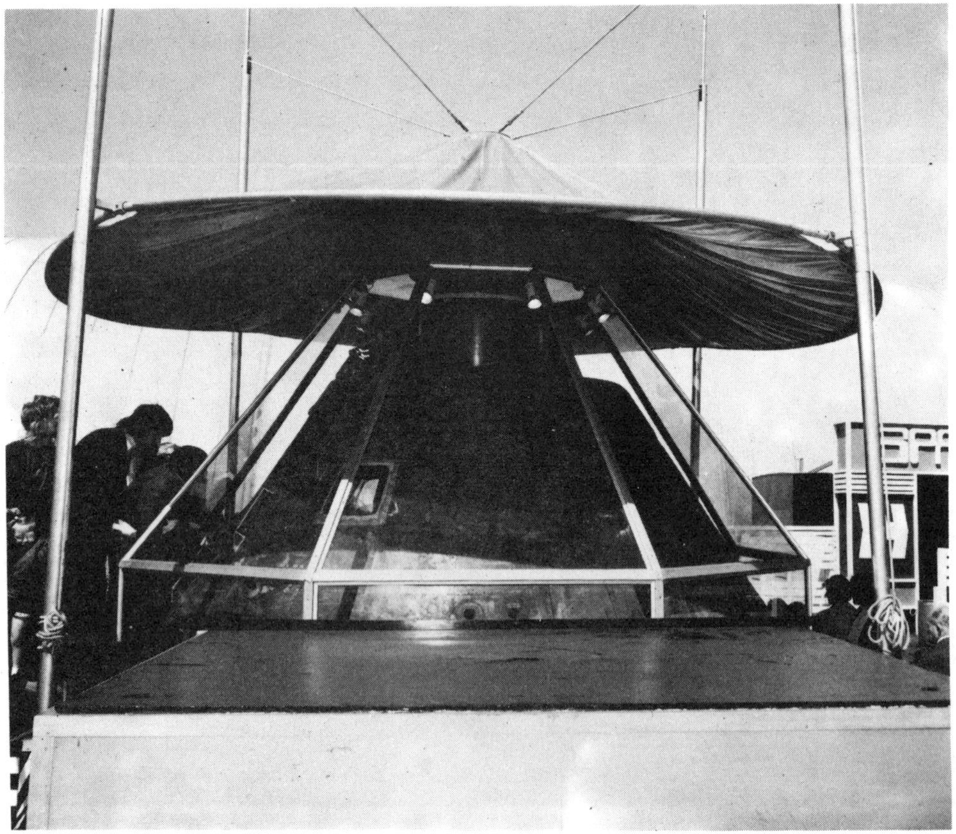

The Arts

The people of Merseyside have always been keen on the arts. The oldest music society in Britain is the **Royal Liverpool Philharmonic Society.** It was established in 1840. A group of music lovers used to meet in various salons. Enthusiasm for their music-making was so great that a fund raised enough money to build an impressive concert hall. In 1933 the original Liverpool Philharmonic Hall was burnt down and the present hall which attracts musicians from all parts of the world, was opened in 1939. The Liverpool Philharmonic Society was given the title "Royal" by the Queen in 1957. The Society's orchestra is known all over the world. Its present conductor is Sir Charles Groves.

Left: Apollo 10 at Liverpool Show 1971.
Middle: Moon rock display at Liverpool Show.
Right: Royal Liverpool Philharmonic Orchestra.

Theatres have also been a tradition in Liverpool. In the 1850's Dickens, the famous novelist, brought a company of actors to perform at the Theatre Royal. The same building later became a cold storage warehouse, but has now been demolished. The **Liverpool Playhouse,** in the shadow of the old Theatre Royal, is one of the oldest repertory theatres in England. It opened in 1911. Famous actors, like Rex Harrison, John Slater and Megs Jenkins, were once members of the Liverpool Playhouse Company. On the corner of Lime Street stands the **Empire Theatre** which has a reputation for musical shows, variety and pantomime. **The Royal Court** also offers a similar entertainment. The Empire and the Royal Court have been places where the great Liverpool comedians like Arthur Askey, Jimmy Tarbuck and Ken Dodd have performed. The **Everyman Theatre** specialises in unusual or modern plays, while the **Neptune,** run by Liverpool Corporation, gives amateurs an opportunity to perform in a good theatre.

Outside Liverpool there is a theatre in St. Helens called the **Theatre Royal** and in Birkenhead there used to be the **Argyle Theatre** which was bombed in 1940 during the Second World War. It was built in 1868 and in its prime the old-fashioned music hall used to flourish to the sound of great comedians like Harry Lauder, Vesta Tilley and Billy Russell.

The Liverpool Playhouse.

Above: One of the very first BBC outside broadcasts from the old Argyle Theatre, Birkenhead.
Right: Liverpool Museum.

Merseyside also has its fair share of Art Galleries and Museums. The **Liverpool Museum** was established in 1860 and the **Walker Art Gallery** (named after Sir Andrew Barclay Walker, a local brewer) has been in existence since 1877. At the Liverpool Museum you can see the relics of Merseyside's past. Two very interesting galleries are the Transport Gallery which houses a steam engine and coaches from the first days of steam and many old horse-drawn vehicles, and the second one is the "History of the Port of Liverpool" Gallery.

The Walker Art Gallery is equally famous. Thousands of people visit the gallery to see the masterpieces from the past. Every year an exhibition, called after a Liverpool businessman, John Moores, is held, of paintings by modern artists like Sam Walsh and Adrian Henri, who live and paint in Liverpool.

The awareness of the arts on Merseyside spreads outside the major city of Liverpool. **The Grosvenor Museum** in Chester, the **Williamson** in Birkenhead, the **Lady Lever Art Gallery** in Ellesmere Port are all worth a visit. There are also historic houses like **Speke Hall** and **Rufford Old Hall.** These places are museums in their own right. A very unusual museum exists in St. Helens. The **Pilkington Glass Museum** has examples of how glass was used in the past and how with some imagination it can be used in the future. One model that has been on show at the Museum showed how glass could be used to build a city in the middle of the North Sea. Who knows? This might not be only a pipe dream. We will have to find more places for people to live if the population increases.

Speke Hall.

A day out

There are also opportunities of going to places like **Chester Zoo** or **Knowsley Safari Park** to see animals. Chester Zoo over the years has become one of the leading zoos in Britain. The Knowsley Safari Park has only been open a few years. It is on Lord Derby's land. The wild animals roam about free and you can only go through the park in a covered vehicle. You are not allowed to leave your car. It could be dangerous.

On Sundays many people in Merseyside go to church. The two most famous churches are the two Cathedrals in Liverpool. The **Anglican Cathedral** is built of rich red sandstone and it rises high over Liverpool on St. James's Mount. The foundation stone was laid on 19th July 1904 by King Edward VII. The architect was Sir Gilbert Scott, who was only twenty-two years of age when he submitted his plans for the Cathedral. The Cathedral has been growing steadily over the past seventy years and it is as yet still unfinished. The architect, **Sir Gilbert Scott,** has long been dead but still the work goes on. There are some stone masons who have spent their entire working life helping to build this Cathedral, which is one of the most impressive churches of modern times. It is hoped that by 1975 the Cathedral will be finished. When you see the huge vaulted roofs, they will take your breath away and the view from the top of the tower is never to be forgotten.

In more recent times the new Metropolitan Roman Catholic Cathedral has shared the skyline with the Anglican Cathedral. It was opened on 14th May 1967, although the foundation stone was laid in June 1933. The modern satellite-shaped cathedral has been built on top of the original crypt and foundations of the cathedral planned in 1933. See if you can find pictures of this original plan; compare the old and the new. It has been designed to reflect the spirit of the space age in which we live. The architect was **Frederick Gibberd** and his design is impressively simple. The interior is circular with the altar in the centre of a large area. High above the congregation a massive crown of coloured glass lets in a splendour of light. You have to look up in this Cathedral to capture the majesty of the building. The two Cathedrals are joined by Hope Street which is a symbol, perhaps, for the religious unity that exists on Merseyside. There are many interesting churches. **The Ancient Chapel of Toxteth** was founded by Richard Mather in 1618. Richard Mather later settled in America to escape from religious persecution in Britain. His story is worth finding out. Some of the Parish Churches near your home may have a long history like **All Saints in Childwall** which is mentioned in William the Conqueror's "Domesday Book". Nearby the church it is thought the Roundheads and the Royalists fought a bloody battle during the Civil War. You may be able to find something about the history of your area from the tombstones in the graveyard of your local church.

The Anglican Cathedral.

E3. The heart of Merseyside in words and song

The Metropolitan Cathedral.

Merseyside has always been famous for its humour, its vital accent and its song. The humour comes from having to face up to many years of poverty. Just over a hundred years ago Liverpool had to set to to look after thousands of hungry Irish families. In the 1940's in Liverpool hundreds of families lost their homes during the bombing. Their strong sense of humour helped them to maintain their high spirits.
The dockers especially have a reputation for their wit. They are always giving each other nicknames. Here are some. Stanley Matthews—he always says "I'll take this corner". Jellipex—because he only has one coat. Spaceman—because he always goes to Ma's for dinner. You may like to compile your own book of dockers' nicknames.

Ships and sailors

The Merseysider has preferred to sing about his troubles than brood over them. Liverpool has a long tradition with the sea and in the old days when sailors met they sang sea shanties. The song may have expressed the joy of returning home to Liverpool after a long voyage.

"Whip Jamboree, Whip Jamboree,
Oh your pig tail sailor, hanging down behind,
Whip Jamboree, Whip Jamboree,
Oh Jenny get your oat cakes done".

The Spinners, the Liverpool folk group, have recorded most of the old sea shanties including "Whip Jamboree". Listen to the whole song and follow the story of the ship's homeward journey into Liverpool. What dock did the ship tie up at? What does the song tell of other Liverpool landmarks?
Other songs about the sea are about sadness, leaving a sweetheart behind, perhaps.

"So fare thee well my own true love
For when I return united we will be,
It's not the leaving of Liverpool that grieves me
But my darling when I think of thee".

Since the early days of sail the songwriters have continued to immortalise people who have since died. **Seth Davy** was one such character. He was a coloured man who was a street entertainer. He used to sit on street corners with dolls on the end of a plank. When he banged one end of the plank the dolls would bounce up and down. To the passers by they looked as if they were dancing.

"He sat on the corner of Bevington Bush
Astride an old packing case,
And the dolls at the end of his plank went
a-dancing
As he crooned with a smile on his face.
Come day, go day
Wish in my heart it was Sunday,
Drinking buttermilk all the week
Whisky on a Sunday.

Seth Davy.

His tired old hands drummed the wooden beam
And the dolls they danced the gear,
A much better show than you ever did see
At the Pivvy or New Brighton Pier.

But in 1902 old Seth Davy died
And his song it was heard no more
And the two dancing dolls in a jigger bin ended,
And the plank went to mend a back door.

On some stormy nights down Scotty Road way
With the wind blowing up from the sea
You can still hear the song of old Seth Davy
As he croons to his dancing dolls three".

The word *"gear"* means *"the best"*.
There are three things you can find out from the words of that song.

1. Find the names mentioned in the song on a map of modern Liverpool.
2. What does the song tell us about the life of the time?
3. What words in the song do you think are special to Liverpool?

There's a place

In the 1960's Liverpool became famous for places made popular by the Beatles, like *Penny Lane* and *Strawberry Fields*. *Penny Lane* is obviously a street, but where is it? Play the record and listen to the words. Make a note of all the people mentioned in the song like the barber and then visit Penny Lane itself. Is the picture the Beatles have drawn accurate?
Strawberry Fields is a home for children run by The Salvation Army. It just goes to show how Merseyside writers like the place where they live. If they hated their home they would not write about it so much.

Old legends

These songs are only part of Merseyside's background. There are also the legends or stories from history that have become part of Merseyside's life. In Hale churchyard you can see the grave of John Middleton, who was born in 1578. He was very tall, over 2 m 82 cm in fact, and because of his height he was called a giant. There are many books which will tell you John Middleton's story and how his fame reached as far as the court of the King of England.

In Wallasey, on the promenade overlooking the Mersey, there is an old house which is now in disrepair. This was Mother Redcap's. Mother Redcap used to keep a public house and she sheltered smugglers from the Customs officers. When Britain was at war with France at the end of the eighteenth century, import taxes were imposed on everything that was brought into the country, especially goods like rum and salt. Because of the taxes, smuggling increased. The smugglers used to hide their rum and salt in the caves under Mother Redcap's public house.
If you look hard enough you will find plenty of stories about the personalities and the dramatic events that have happened on Merseyside. Although these are now in the past they have all contributed to making Merseyside what it is today. Here are just a few names and events to start you off.
Kitty Wilkinson was a remarkable woman. She fought to build wash-houses for poor people to use.
In 1955 a French acrobatic parachutist plunged to his death during a show held at Speke Airport.
What about these names from further back in Merseyside's history: Sarah Biffin, William Roscoe, William Gladstone and Silas K. Hocking?

Scouse

A Merseysider also has his own way of speaking. Liverpool especially is famous for its language of "scouse" as it is usually called. The Liverpudlian's dictionary would look something like this:—

Wet Nelly	a soft, doughy cake
Jigger	a narrow back entry
Scuffer	a policeman
Oller	a bomb site
Whacker	a Liverpool person
Under the arm	inferior quality
The gear	great, fantastic

Make up a dictionary of your own of Liverpool words and phrases.

E4. Away from it all

From time to time, especially in the summer, people who live on Merseyside like to escape from the busy streets. Before the car and the aeroplane were invented people could only travel by horse, by rail or by sea. In days past most ordinary working people could not afford to travel out of town. Holidays were out of the question. This meant they had to relax in places near their homes. To put matters right, Liverpool City Council set out parks on the outskirts of the city boundaries as they existed then. One of the most famous parks in Liverpool is **Sefton Park.**
In 1867 a prize of 300 guineas was offered for the best design. Twenty-nine competitors entered and the prize was awarded jointly to Monsieur André, a landscape gardener from Paris, and Mr. Hornblower, an architect from Liverpool. In the same year, 1867, **Stanley Park** was planned. On 4th December 1867 the City Council decided to employ 1000 men to work on laying out the parks. Each workman was to receive not more than two shillings (10p) a day as wages.
On 14th May 1870 Stanley Park was opened and in 1872 Sefton Park welcomed His Royal Highness Prince Arthur, the third son of Queen Victoria, to perform the opening ceremony. People travelled from all over Liverpool to the parks. They visited places like the Palm House in Sefton Park where they could see strange tropical plants growing in the steamy atmosphere. Find out more about

The Palm House, Sefton Park.

The Palm House, Sefton Park.

parks near your home like Arrowe Park and Birkenhead Park, Walton Hall Park and Reynolds Park. Study carefully the architecture of the buildings in the parks. Is it similar? If it is, what does it tell you about the architectural taste of our forefathers?

Holidays

Later, the Wirral became more populated. Places like New Brighton became popular holiday resorts. The roundabouts, fairgrounds and sideshows provided a cheap popular day out for the poor families of Liverpool. The frequent ferry service made it easy for the holidaymakers to cross the Mersey. Later still, the opening of the railway under the Mersey to the Wirral offered an alternative for those who wanted to visit New Brighton without using the ferry.
When the car was invented, only the rich could afford to buy the early models. The roads were not built for cars. The more wealthy people on Merseyside in the first thirty years of this century travelled to the Isle of Man on a fleet of ships built up by the **Isle of Man Steam Ship Company.** The famous ships with red and black funnels all had names connected with the Isle of Man. 'The Lady of Man', 'Tynwald', 'Manx Maid' and 'Snaefell' are all names that have graced the Isle of Man Steam Ship Company. Some of these ships have long since been broken up, but ships still ply between the Mersey and the island.
Can you find the names of the ships that are still in service. Some ships make the journey all the year round, while others are laid up in the winter and are only brought into service for the summer season. Find out the names of the ships that are in service all through the year and those which are only used in the summer.
Since the Second World War the Isle of Man has become less popular with Merseysiders as a traditional holiday resort. The heyday of the Isle

of Man is now over though, compared with the prosperous twenties and thirties when thousands of Merseysiders automatically made it their first holiday choice.
People want to travel farther to make sure of finding the sun. There are those who remain loyal to the island. Many of them have been going there every year since they were children. School children from Merseyside schools still enjoy camping in schools during the summer holidays on the island.
Between the First and Second World Wars, in the 1920's and 30's, the car was getting more popular. Cars were being mass produced and therefore much cheaper. Even those who still could not afford cars made trips to the country-side by motor coach. Wales became popular as a place for a day out especially when the Mersey Tunnel was opened in 1934. The Crosville Motor Services Company opened up regular services between Birkenhead and Loggerheads near Mold at this time. At Loggerheads the day-trippers could enjoy walks and there was a tea garden for the less-energetic.
People were looking farther afield. They were finding more opportunities to escape from the back streets. Young people joined the Youth Hostel Association and others took to their bicycles in their hundreds.
As more families could afford motor cars they became independent. They did not have to wait any longer for a train, bus or ferry. Today distance is no object and it is difficult to pinpoint the places where Merseysiders spend their holidays. The traditional resorts like New Brighton and the Isle of Man have declined.
In recent years there has also been an increase in the number of people flying. Today thousands of passengers board airliners for holidays in the sun in Spain or Yugoslavia.
The speed of travel has affected our lives. A hundred years ago, it would have taken a family two hours to travel eight miles from Walton, in the North of Liverpool, to Sefton Park, in the South. Now it takes only two hours to travel from Liverpool to the Costa Brava in Spain.
Travel has broadened the Merseysider's outlook. He is no longer trapped in dingy back streets. He can take his children out to explore far afield.

Holidaymakers boarding I.O.M. boat.

E5. Being in the know

People on Merseyside need to know what is going on. To meet this need there are many organisations which supply information and news. Most people learn about what is going on on Merseyside from newspapers, radio and television. Merseyside has two big newspapers which cover the area, the **Liverpool Daily Post,** which comes out every week-day morning and the **Liverpool Echo** which appears on the streets in the evening.
The staff of a newspaper is divided into various sections. There are the *reporters* who go out to find news about what is happening minute by minute every day. If a bus crashes through a shop window in the main street, the reporter will be on the scene in minutes, making shorthand notes which he will later use to write a report to appear within hours in the next edition.
The reporter's work is important because he keeps the community up to date with what is happening.
A *feature writer* does not work on up-to-minute news. He will write about topics of special interest. The *Editor* is the man who decides what is going into the paper. If he decides to ask a feature writer to enquire into "Schools on Merseyside" for example, the feature writer will then spend perhaps three or four days interviewing headmasters, teachers, parents and pupils. His feature will be published a week later.
Other journalists specialise in particular interests. There are people who write on fashion, gardening, cars, sport, drama, the arts and many other subjects which readers find interesting.

If a subject is popular, it might be covered regularly.
Most towns on Merseyside have local newspapers. **The Southport Visitor, St. Helens Reporter, Liverpool Weekly News, Ellesmere Port Pioneer.** Can you complete the list? Look up your telephone directory under place names and find out how many newspapers you can find listed. You will notice all these local papers are weeklies. Why is this do you think?
There are some newspapers which are run by groups of residents to express their own views about problems which affect their particular locality. **The Scottie Press,** the **Free Press** and the **Tuebrook Bugle** belong to this group.

Local radio

Ever since November 1967, Merseyside has had its own local radio station. It is run by the **British Broadcasting Corporation.** The studios are situated in the middle of Liverpool. The programmes are beamed from the studio to a tall transmitters on Allerton Golf Course, one of the highest points around Liverpool and at Wallasey. The programmes are then transmitted to a distance of roughly thirty miles around Liverpool. You can find a complete list of programmes broadcast by **BBC Radio Merseyside** in the *Radio Times.* Study them carefully and ask yourself why certain programmes are broadcast at certain times of the day. Why are news and topical programmes broadcast between six and nine a.m. and topical programmes for women broadcast every week-day between 10.30 and 11 a.m.?
BBC Radio Merseyside comes on the air at 6.30 a.m. and the station produces an average of eleven hours of local programmes per day. Each day starts with the producer, the news man and the presenter arriving at 6 a.m. The reporters from the night before have left taped interviews for the presenter to introduce. Each tape has a cue sheet which looks like this:—

LIVERPOOL STRIKE, 4th JANUARY, A.M.
CONTINUITY: *A lightning strike called by production staff halted work at the Liverton Footwear Factory last night. Our reporter, Walter James, went along to talk to the Works Convener, Mr. Bill Smith. Walter James first asked Mr. Smith what was the cause of the strike. . . .*
Tape Duration: 3·02 minutes.
CONTINUITY: Walter James reporting from Liverton Footwear Factory.

The producer gives the tapes to the presenter in the order in which they are to be played. The producer directs the programme from the control room. The control room is next to the studio. It has a large window through which the producer can see what is going on in the studio.

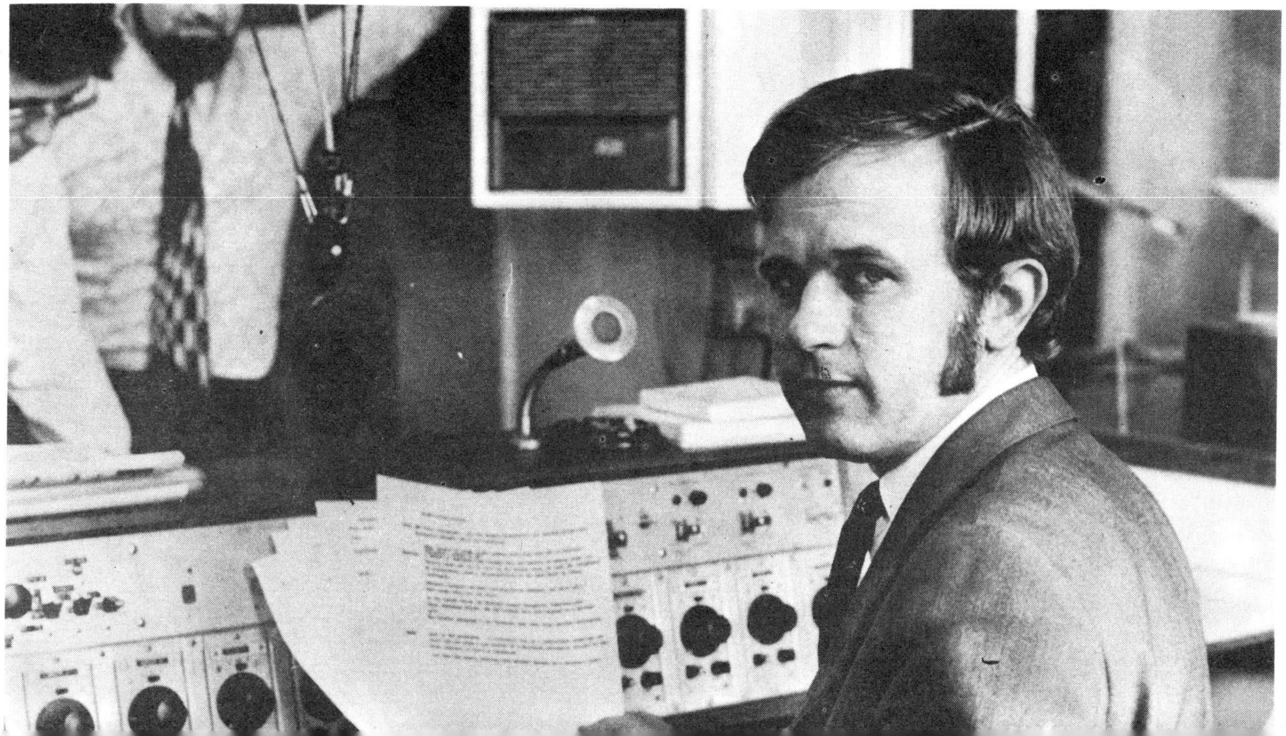

A B.B.C. Radio Merseyside news reader.

Meanwhile other people in the control room are operating the microphones and working the tape-recorders. News men are reading the latest news sent up from London on a special tele-printer in the nearby news room. Local news bulletins are compiled. The presenter frequently tells the time. Why do you think this is?
Each programme is devised by its own producer. Just as journalists specialise on newspapers, so each producer will have his own special interest. Some specialise in news. Others spend their time producing general interest programmes like music and talks, and the Education Department makes programmes for schools and adults.
There are other people called Station Assistants on a Local Radio Station. These are people who make sure that the programmes follow each other smoothly. This is called continuity. The Station Assistants set up the tapes, operate the controls and introduce the programmes by reading the cue sheet. If anything goes wrong with the machines, then the engineers are on the spot. You can find out more about your Local Radio Station. You may be able to arrange a school visit to the studios to see for yourself.

Dial a friend

Another means of communication is the telephone. The telephone system allows people to talk to each other and to pass on personal news between friends and families as opposed to the public news that the radio and newspapers give out. There is also an information service offered by the Post Office. You can get in touch with organisations which can give you valuable local information. The Automobile Association gives road reports to drivers travelling long distances. What other organisations can you telephone for information you may need? A telephone directory will help you.

Merseyside does not have its own local television programmes although the North-West is covered by the Manchester studios and Liverpool sometimes is mentioned.
In a large area like Merseyside communications are important. The area has now become a metropolitan area under one local government body. The old councils like Liverpool and Bootle

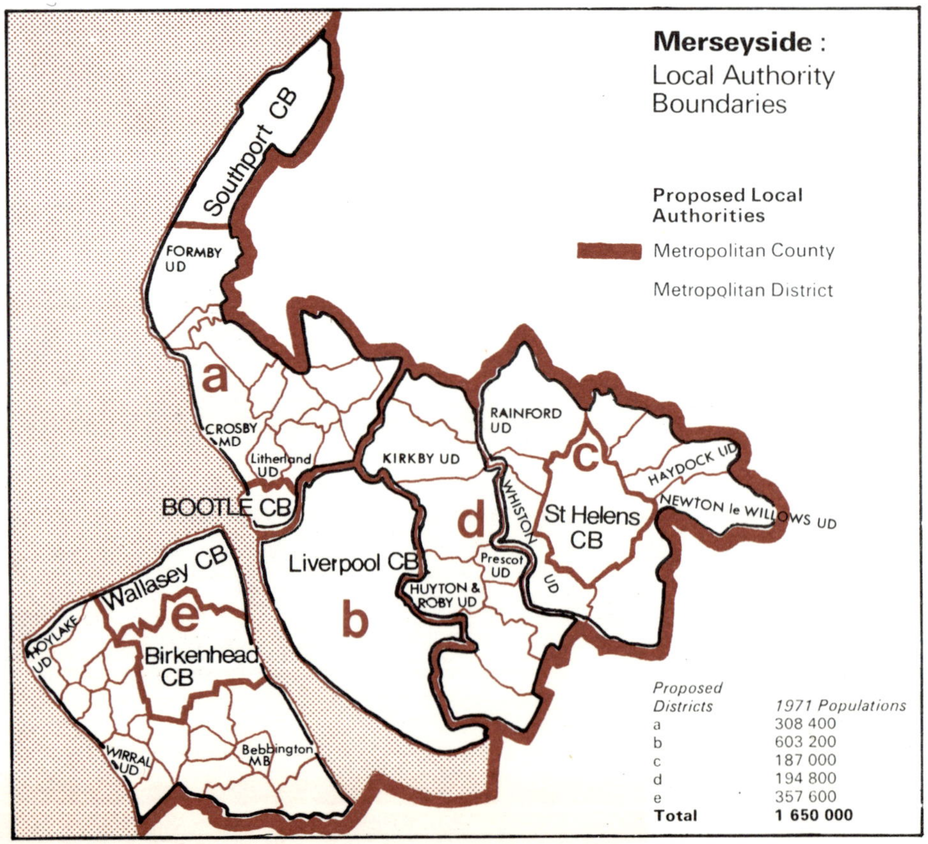

New local government districts.